50

for YOUR FUTURE

50

for YOUR
FUTURE

lessons from
down the road

TAVIS SMILEY

New York Times best-selling author of *What I Know for Sure*

Distributed in the United States by: Hay House, Inc.: www.hayhouse.com® •
Published and distributed in Australia by: Hay House Australia Pty. Ltd.:
www.hayhouse.com.au • Published and distributed in the United Kingdom by:
Hay House UK, Ltd.: www.hayhouse.co.uk • Published and distributed in the
Republic of South Africa by: Hay House SA (Pty), Ltd.: www.hayhouse.co.za •
Distributed in Canada by: Raincoast Books: www.raincoast.com • Published in
India by: Hay House Publishers India: www.hayhouse.co.in

DESIGN: Karla Baker
INTERIOR IMAGES: Shutterstock

Library of Congress Cataloging-in-Publication Data:

Smiley, Tavis, date.
  50 for your future : lessons from down the road / Tavis Smiley.
    pages cm
  ISBN 978-1-4019-4839-9 (hardcover : alk. paper) 1. Conduct of life. I. Title. II.
Title: Fifty for your future.
  BJ1589.S646 2016
  170'.44--dc23

                    2015012761

Hardcover ISBN: 978-1-4019-4839-9
10 9 8 7 6 5 4 3 2
1st edition, April 2016
Printed in the United States of America

SUSTAINABLE
FORESTRY
INITIATIVE
Certified Chain of Custody
Promoting Sustainable Forestry
www.sfiprogram.org
SFI-01268

SFI label applies to the text stock

table *of* CONTENTS

introduction

This book is about trying, failing, and, in the words of the great playwright Samuel Beckett, "failing better"! Inside you'll find 50 lessons that I'm grateful to have learned over the years, a multitude of which have found their way into the many commencement addresses I've had the honor to deliver over the course of my broadcast career.

I thought it might be of some value to put on paper what I hope have served as insights and inspirations to others.

We hear all the time "I wish I knew then what I know now." I do as well! But I've come to understand that there's no way for me to have known then what I've been able to gain over the years through experience—through the process of just living life.

I'm not so naive to think that simply sharing these lessons with you is going to magically change your life. All of us have to go through an individual process, of traveling down whatever our road may be, and learn the lessons unique to each of us—and by the best means possible.

I do, though, believe in sharing wisdom and knowledge, and that there is power that can be gained through that sharing. I believe that the more you know, the more you grow. And I believe that no good experience ought to be wasted.

In that spirit, then, this book may have a longer shelf life than most. This may be a book that you come back to from time to time. It may be a book that doesn't completely make sense or resonate with you right now, but hopefully will later on.

And aren't we all familiar with that? It was funny to me how many of these lessons caused me to flash back to something my parents had tried to tell me, or what other, wiser friends and mentors hoped to impart to me when I was younger.

I still had to learn things in my own way.

My hope is that these lessons will be of help both to those folks just stepping out into the world on their own for the first time, as well as readers who, like me, are a bit more chronologically gifted with more years to look back on!

Some of these lessons I learned early on. Some of these lessons I learn perennially. Some I'm just now beginning to fully grasp. Still, some of these lessons will be ones that I hope steer you away from making mistakes. Others just offer a heads up—they are unavoidable. Some will be lessons to help you deal honestly with other people, and teach you how to focus on and deal better with yourself.

In truth, I'm still learning lessons every day.

I'm still making mistakes, and I'm still learning from them. I'm still falling and floundering and failing, but I'm also still growing and moving forward.

Through it all, I'm still searching for the truth, for the grace notes in life, applying the lessons I learned that will assure that the years to come are even more successful, fruitful, meaningful, and dynamic.

TAVIS SMILEY
Los Angeles, CA
Winter 2015

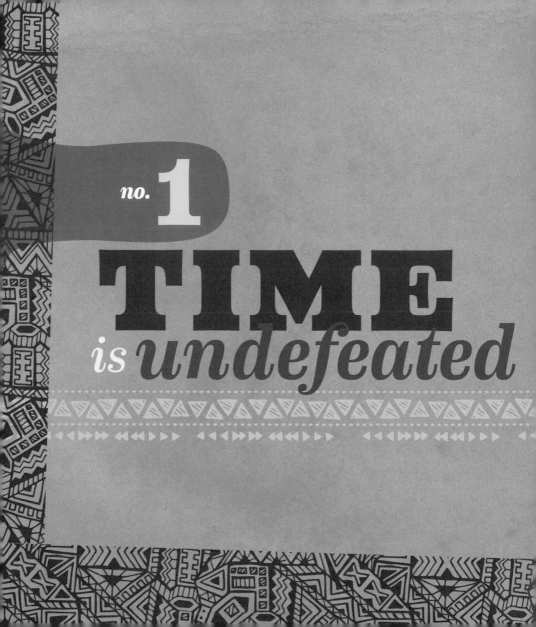

no. **1**

TIME
is undefeated

When I turned 35 I had an epiphany.

I suspect at some point you'll have this epiphany too, and if you haven't experienced it already, I hope you'll be lucky enough to be as young as I was when it happened to me. I was giving a major speech when I was 35, in which I noted that based on the average life expectancy for a Black male at that time, I had more of my life behind me than in front of me.

My epiphany was this: At the rate I'm going, I'm not going to win this battle with time. So from that moment on, I picked up my pace, made better choices, and didn't waste time or treasure on insignificant things.

I got much more serious about my hustle.

I'm sure we've all heard that 40 is the new 30, or that 50 is the new 40. I'm here to tell you it's a lie! Contrary to what the talking heads in the media or the advertising execs want us to believe, 50 is the same old 50, and 40 is the same old 40. Nobody says that 90 is the new 80. You know why? Because when you're 90, you're just 90!

I've come to accept all of this for what it means—that time has control over us and not the other way around. I'm doing all I can to reach 90, but the reality is you've got less time than you think—and less time than what Madison Avenue wants you to believe! The sooner every one of us stops buying into this nonsense, the better off we'll be.

Now, this *is* true: Life expectancy is increasing, medicine is always making impressive advancements, and many of us have committed to healthier diets and more physical exercise.

And yet there is still no guarantee that you're going to live a long life. That's what they don't tell you: You could still get cancer, have a heart attack, or get into an accident of some kind.

We can do all the right things to reduce these risks—and we should—but there's not much we can do to eliminate them altogether. There's a reason physicians are in the practice of medicine—they're still *practicing*.

In truth, we don't control when we come into the world, and we

don't control when—or how—we leave it. We don't control when we die, where we die, or how we die.

The only thing we control is what we live for. I'd rather live for a cause, than just because.

None of us escapes life alive. We all know what's coming—why not make the most of every precious bit of time we're given?

no. 2

when
your
LIFE
exceeds
your
dreams,

DREAM
BIGGER
DREAMS

I remember watching *BROADCAST NEWS*

▶ ◀◀◀▶▶▶ ◀◀◀◀▶▶▶ ◀◀

when the movie came out in 1987. The film focuses on a talented if emotionally unstable television news producer and the two rival reporters—one brilliant but abrasive, the other charismatic but inexperienced—working for her. At one point the character played by William Hurt asks, "What do you do when your real life exceeds your dreams?"

That question struck me. At the time, my life hadn't necessarily exceeded my dreams. But I remember thinking that I would love to have that happen to me.

And then one day it did.

As I child I was always dreaming about the future. I dreamt about growing up to play first base for the Cincinnati Reds' "Big Red Machine." I envisioned going on tour with the Jackson 5. My brothers and I would improvise gospel sermons and try to out-preach each other, imagining we were revivalists on the road to save souls. I even fantasized about being the first Black senator from Indiana in the United States Congress.

Little did I know that one day I would get to a place where my life really *would* exceed my own dreams.

What I've learned along the way is this: For that to happen, you have to set your intentions so high that people laugh at you when you share them. People ought to cock their heads and look at you funny. They should be telling you to dial it back, to tone it down, to pump your brakes.

If you share your dream and people say, "That's nice. That's cute. That's sweet" and just pat you on the head, then you're dreaming discounted dreams.

Your dreams should be so big that they shock people into backing up when they hear what you're planning.

When I was a child, it scared me to think that by the time I got to be an adult, there'd be nothing left to do. Everything seemed to be getting done already; there were innovations, creations, and inventions, one after another.

Lord, how wrong I was.

There's still so much that vexes the spirit, that burdens the soul, that holds people back, that denies opportunity, that keeps humanity as a whole from advancing. By all accounts, the realm of dreams is limitless. Dream what you want the world to be—what you want for your life—and commit yourself to the task. Make it a point to out-dream yourself!

In my offices in Los Angeles, this question is posted everywhere: *What is the next big thing?* That's the question I'm always looking to answer. I want to do something that hasn't been done before, or in a different way than it's ever been done, or in a place where no one had ever imagined it being done before, or applied in a different way than anyone else has ever tried before.

You want to find yourself routinely dreaming bigger dreams—to find yourself reaching your distant goals, crashing through them, and rising to the next level.

Because the answer to the question in *Broadcast News*—and in life in general—is that when your life exceeds your dreams, dream bigger dreams!

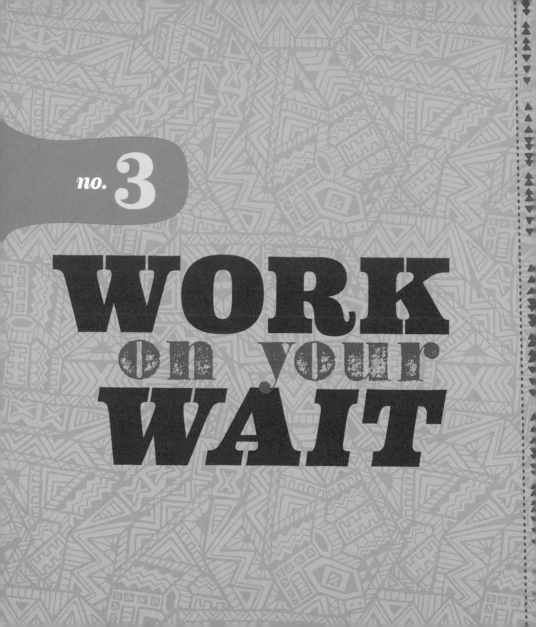

no. **3**

WORK on your WAIT

For much of my life, I believed patience was overrated.

When I attended Indiana University, I was "Mr. Involved." Debate team, student associations, fraternity life, volunteer work, two work-study jobs, internships—you name it, I did it!

One of those internships brought me to Los Angeles the summer before my senior year, to intern for then-mayor Tom Bradley. I quickly fell in love with Los Angeles and the idea of working full-time for Mayor Bradley, who became one of the great mentors in my life. I was ready to quit college, move to California, and get started on a career in politics. I knew what I wanted, and I was ready to go!

Mayor Bradley taught me an invaluable lesson at that time: You have to work on your wait. He counseled me to return to Indiana to finish school. He promised to find me a spot in his administration after I graduated. And he stayed true to his word.

Mayor Bradley wasn't looking to quash the enthusiasm and ambition he saw burning in me. He was trying to teach me to value and trust the maturation process.

As I mentioned earlier, we live in a world that tells us: "Get your hustle on." That message is loudest for young people.

That's not necessarily a bad thing. Having goals and drive are essential. But you still don't go from intern to chairman of the board—or mayor of Los Angeles, for that matter—overnight. Patience keeps us in the game. It gives us the focus to prevent small failures from becoming total defeat, and the mindfulness to put opportunities and victories in perspective. It's believing in and trusting the process. Following it will often get you where you want to go.

But patience is only as helpful as the effort you put into it. That's why you have to *work* on your wait— not just wait!

When you see an article, a show, or a post about a James or a Zuckerberg or a Jay Z, it can seem as though they became successful overnight. The truth is that there are years of work and effort, ups and downs, behind those successes.

Look at LeBron! Sure, he was drafted into the NBA right out of high school, but only because he spent the previous ten years of his life playing in every basketball game he could find, going to every practice, and *patiently* doing everything he could to make himself a great player.

And although it may seem that Pharrell Williams became an instant success in 2013 with his hit song "Happy," he had put years of hard work into the music business by collaborating behind the scenes with other artists on their albums before being offered his own record contract and becoming a household name.

I have learned that there is no substitute for doing the work, and no skipping steps in "the process." Learning to work on your wait helps prepare you for the long-distance race that is life.

no. **4**

you
can't
FIT IN
and
STAND
OUT

I love *jazz.*

The music provides one of the rare experiences where you can actually fit in and stand out at the same time. The genius of any great jazz band is found not only in the mellifluous sound of the ensemble as a whole, but also when the individual musicians step out in front to solo.

Life for the rest of us isn't always so jazzlike, however.

If you're trying to fit in with the crowd, it's hard to stand out. It's difficult to be a conformist and a trendsetter at the same time. You'll get noticed only if you create your own signature sound or discover your own unique style.

I have a friend who currently lives in a conservative community in Southern California. In her younger years, she was a liberal political activist. She worked for Senator Robert Kennedy when he ran for president on the Democratic ticket in 1968, and she was even at the Ambassador Hotel in Los Angeles the tragic night he was assassinated. Back then, my friend stood out as an individual with integrity who could think for herself.

But once she moved to a place that didn't embrace her beliefs, she gradually began to change. It took a number of years, but she made the decision to fit in with her new conservative neighbors rather than hold fast to her true ideals and risk social isolation.

Think about the people you admire or hold in high regard in your own life. They certainly didn't reach the heights of their success or significance by simply being a member of the human herd, an ordinary follower in an unimaginative life.

Do you really think you're going to make your mark in the world by simply "fitting in"? You're not.

And just so we're clear, know that you can't buy integrity. Amazon can't ship it, Netflix doesn't stream it, and iTunes won't let you download it.

No, integrity comes only from having the courage to keep an unwavering commitment to your convictions.

I've discovered in life that, whether people like you or loathe you, whether they love you or hate you, whether they get you or not, they'll *respect* you for being true to your convictions and beliefs. For standing out.

At the end of the day, what are you really after? To be accepted or to be respected? If you're just looking to be liked, then go ahead—it's very easy to fit in.

But if you're looking for respect, then live your life based on your principles. Live your life on your own terms.

no. 5

DO WHAT YOU *believe,* **NOT WHAT YOU FIND EXPEDIENT**

If I were to ask you right now what your personal mission statement is, what would you say?

Just like institutions, organizations, and corporations, each of us has to create and implement a mission statement for our own lives. It can't be something you read in a book, something you overheard, something suggested *to* you, or just the same thing everyone around you seems to believe. What is it *you* believe?

When you have a mission statement for your life, when you have your own belief system, it makes navigating everything else in life so much easier. This applies especially when a crisis comes your way, when situations develop, when challenge confronts you, or when you're stuck with a conundrum about how you're going to address life's difficult issues. Those who have a belief system—whose lives are grounded in a mission statement—tend to find problems easier to navigate because, regardless of what's confronting them, their answer can always begin with: "Here's what I believe about this . . ."

Absent these guiding principles, which act as an operating manual for your life, too often the tendency— the default setting—is to take the most expedient route, the path of least resistance. Many times this means simply borrowing the beliefs or ideas or decisions of others, which is a step toward letting the outside world put a bid on your soul.

Your mission statement should be like the secret password for your life.

It will help you keep secure everything that's precious.

My mission statement is to do my small part to make the world safe for the legacy of Dr. Martin Luther King, Jr., which is "justice for all, service to others, and a love that liberates people."

I've made this my life's mission because I believe the very future of American democracy is inextricably linked to how seriously we take the lessons of his legacy. Why is it so important? Because it teaches us the only way we will ever effectively deal with what Dr. King called the triple threat facing American democracy: racism, poverty, and militarism.

The three issues Dr. King spoke about 50 years ago remain the same three issues that still threaten to tear apart this country today.

So no matter how people see me—as a media personality, author, or social advocate—wherever I am, whatever I'm doing, I'm working my hustle at every level toward the goal of upholding that mission statement.

I ask the question again: What's yours? Crafting your belief system isn't an overnight process. But as with so much else in life, there's nothing to stop you from beginning today, and no reason to wait any longer to do it.

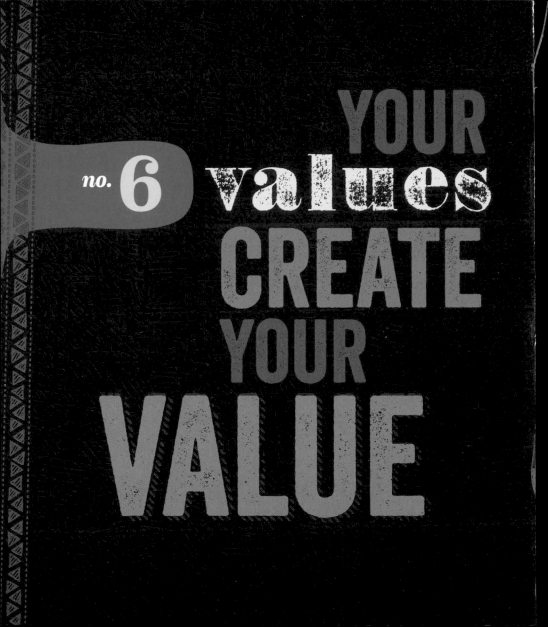

no. **6**

YOUR

values

CREATE

YOUR

VALUE

The letters all start out the same:
"Tavis, I adore you. I watch you
every night on PBS . . ."
"I TiVo your show if I have to miss it . . ."
"You're the best thing on television . . ."

They always start out so beautifully. And then they all move on to the same point, the one thing they can't understand: "Why is your show sponsored by Walmart?"

Familiar arguments and objections about Walmart follow: They're local "job killers" when they open in a small town, they exercise bad labor practices, they negatively impact local and independent businesses.

I've actually drafted a form letter in response to this specific concern. I tell these folks that I'm not ashamed to have been sponsored by Walmart for the past two decades.

The corporation has never once pressured me about my programming or tried to influence my coverage in any way, shape, or form.

I also include a profoundly important lesson I've learned over the years:

Every one of us is compromised in some way.

By the world, by ourselves, or by our associations. But this doesn't mean we can't still have integrity.

In terms of Walmart and my show, my point is that no company is perfect. If I'd waited for a perfect sponsor for my show, I'd still be waiting to get on the air.

So I'm compromised; I'm an American working in the American media, and I need money to do what I am called to do. Walmart provides it to me, and in return I have absolute creative autonomy with my guests, my topics of discussion, and the variety and range of perspectives I'm privileged to share with my viewers.

If you watch my show, you know that I work to impart truth every single night. You're getting something that you won't find elsewhere. You're being exposed to ideas that would otherwise evade you. I'm trying, in love, to challenge you to reexamine the assumptions you hold, to expand your inventory of ideas, and to view my show as a platform where American voices are freely exchanged.

I believe there is value in that. So, despite my compromised status, I'm still doing my best to act with integrity in this world.

As people searching for our vocations and callings in life and working to refine our inherent gifts, we all try to balance our sense of truth with the reality of our lives. I believe very strongly in right and wrong. When I was a child, I believed that there was *only* right or wrong. If it wasn't true, it must be a lie. As I've gotten older, I've come to understand that there is *the* truth, and there is a way *to* the truth. You never know where any given person is on his or her journey toward personal revelation. On my path, I gradually became aware of gray areas within the concept of truth— nothing is simply black or white, and there's freedom in allowing ideas to exist in a swirling sphere of constant change.

That's why you must never, ever act like or believe you have a monopoly on the truth—we are all compromised. This doesn't mean you shouldn't seek truth, speak truth, or stand on truth. Life will constantly try to get us to make concessions; it happens so frequently, we can at times feel like we're stuck in a quagmire of compromises. Integrity is our lifeline out.

no. 7

THERE IS
no
REBATE FOR
SELLING YOUR
SOUL

My good friend the brilliant comedian Katt Williams

was at my house one day and we were having a conversation about truth telling.

I love comedy. I also think the best comedians take very seriously their ability to use their medium to tell us many uncomfortable, inconvenient, unsettling truths. In that department, Katt is one of the best.

Our conversation centered on his unique gift. Comedians have the opportunity to make us laugh, oftentimes at ourselves, all the while imparting sacred truths about topics the rest of us rarely have the courage to discuss.

During that conversation Katt said he was inspired by my work—a very generous comment—because he perceives me as telling hard truths in my own straightforward way on a regular basis.

He said to me, "Every time I watch you work or we hang out and talk, I'm always brought back to this point: There is no rebate for selling your soul."

To put it a different way, I've learned that there is no substitute for telling the truth.

Truth is like a line of credit that keeps you from ever having to sell your soul.

I cannot overstate the importance of this. You must not sell your soul. You can't surrender your soul, and you can't let this world steal it. Your soul is the most precious commodity you have, and it has to be protected at all costs.

I'm not talking about your spirit here. Your spirit can wander, have changes of opinion, or lead you in one direction or another. Your soul, on the other hand, is the essence of who you are.

I believe that there are manipulative spirits all around us, competing for influence over our souls. I find that I need a hedge of protection from them, so I turn to my personal beliefs to help me.

But regardless of your religious convictions, I can tell you for certain that our souls are constantly under attack by plenty of secular spirits too. People around us are negative. People gossip. Others will lie to us. Some folks want to trip us up or set us up.

All these spirits are coming at us every day. And they're all after the same thing: your soul. Lobbyists are after the souls of politicians. Drug dealers are after the souls of users. Madison Avenue is after all our souls—it tries to hypnotize us into believing we're less than ideal so we'll buy products we don't need!

We can guard our souls by being truth tellers, by following our beliefs and not simply doing what's easy or convenient, by not squandering the gifts we were born with, by living with a righteous rage.

And by learning how to do this early on.

Because once they've got your soul . . . it's game over.

no. **8**

some
years
ASK
questions,
some
years
GIVE
ANSWERS

Unlike most people, who make resolutions on New Year's Eve,

I make mine on September 13th, my birthday. Each year, I do the same two things on that day. First, I spend a good portion of it alone, reflecting on what happened the previous year. Second, I write down in a notebook the goals I have for the year to come. I always have two sets of goals: an "internal" set that relates to my spirit, my soul, my character; and an "external" set for my professional career.

As I journey through the year I keep a running tally on how I'm doing on my professional goals, and I try to be mindful of the progress I'm making on my inner life.

What I've learned through this personal "annual review" is that there are years that ask questions, and then there are years that answer them. I've come to realize that often, if I come up short on answers in one year, the next year will satisfy every question that comes my way. I never know what a year might hold.

We live in a world where everyone wants answers, but we never want to wrestle with the questions. Instant gratification can get the best of us— our culture teaches us to cave in to impatience and to take the easy way out instead of patiently searching for deeper meaning. What we don't realize is that sometimes the answers bring with them more questions, and these often present themselves as gifts in disguise.

We don't know what the universe has in store for us. So whatever questions, whatever challenges are thrown at us in a given year, we've got to learn to roll with them.

When I put together my yearly list, I jot down a whole host of things that I want to accomplish. At the time I write it, it always seems like a good and achievable plan. But many times my good intentions are tripped up by dangers, conundrums, and crises that I eventually have to manage, and that I couldn't have seen coming.

U.S. presidents may provide the extreme example of how this happens. Campaign promises inevitably erode in the face of crises that pop up seemingly just as soon as the candidate is elected. I'm always amazed by how quickly presidents have to come to terms with the difference between campaigning and governing. Bush didn't see 9/11 coming; Obama didn't see ISIS, nor did he plan on having to govern under a Republican-led Congress.

What these years full of questions really do is test me. What kind of life am I going to live? What kind of legacy do I want to leave? What kind of human being will I be in the end? Who am I, really?

I've had many years where this type of question just kept coming at me. Once it happened for seven straight years, nonstop. One of the keys to sorting through the questions is to not let them consume you. Throughout those uncertain years, I was still finding success, having important personal moments, and making significant contributions. I wasn't just sitting around vexed and perplexed.

With every Challenge that came along, I said, "Bring it on."

You have to find your own ways of answering the questions, whatever they happen to be. If you're diagnosed with a major illness, that's life asking you, "Now, how are you going to deal with this?" If you lose your job, the question is "Now, what's your next move?" These questions are testing your faith, testing your perseverance, testing your principles, testing your soul.

When people say, "Man, I can't *wait* for this year to be over," what they're really saying is "It's been a year full of unanswered questions."

We can't be afraid of having question years. Anyone who's successful will tell you that they learn more from failures than from successes. The years that ask questions are the years that end up leading to growth. When you embrace those trying years, as with any other test, there's a reward once you finish— there are answers waiting for you on the other side.

no. 9

SOMETIMES YOU LEAD LIKE A GENERAL.

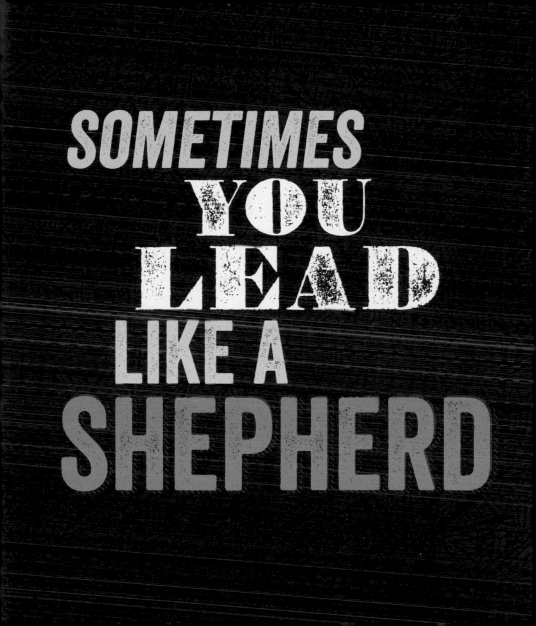

I'VE BEEN A leader IN SOME WAY, SHAPE, OR FORM my whole life

—from being student body president in high school, to a student senator at Indiana University, to an aide in the mayor's office in Los Angeles, to running my own company. I remain ever-curious about other people's leadership principles. In both my home and office, I have shelves packed with biographies and memoirs of accomplished and inspiring people. I'm drawn to their stories because I want to better understand their philosophies, practices, principles, and theories. I want to become a more effective leader in all the work I do.

After a lot of thinking about it, I've decided the best definition of what it takes to be a leader is this: You can't lead people unless you love people, and you can't save people unless you serve people.

If you want to be a leader or already think yourself a leader, ask yourself these two questions: What is the depth of your love for everyday people? What is the quality of the service you provide to them?

The answers to these questions speak partially to your effectiveness as a leader. Over time, though, I've learned that there's another component to leadership—conduct. I've come to appreciate that sometimes you need to lead like a general, and sometimes you should lead like a shepherd.

In 2011, as he was preparing to commit the U.S. military in Libya, President Obama was heavily criticized for saying he wanted to "lead from behind." I may or may not have agreed with him on how to handle that situation, but I took the time to consider what he might have meant. A lot of people were mocking that notion and saying that you couldn't lead from behind.

Yes, you can! Shepherds do it every day.

The long-term effects of intervention notwithstanding, Obama ultimately kept America out of a ground war in Libya. As a leader, you don't always want to go charging, full gallop, into every situation. Sometimes the best course of action is to lead gently, like a shepherd—and shepherds rarely work alone. This means you bring your team in with you. You empower them to lead, to do what needs to be done, and you support them in their efforts.

This approach can work in your personal, professional, or civic life.

Now, there are absolutely going to be times when you need to lead like a general—when you need to be the one conducting traffic, making decisions, dictating directions. You'll be in the front with the baton waving high. Often, when I'm meeting with my television, radio, and publishing teams, I'm leading like a general: This is what I want to do, this is how I want to do it, this is how I'd like you to handle it.

Being able to discern when you need a soft touch versus when a heavy hand will be more effective is key to great leadership.

Understanding that sometimes you're bound to lose shows a depth of maturity. A leader has to be able to accept any outcome, and to regroup, reconsider, and recover.

But if you have the right team around you and you deploy the right strategy—shepherd or general—you put yourself in a much better position to win.

no. 10

HARMONIZE
YOUR
dissonance

FOR years

I have chosen not to listen to friends and family who tell me that I need more balance in my life. One of the reasons is because balance, by definition, means that things are equal. And there are very few things in my life that are equal.

I don't want to live a life of calm equilibrium. I want to live a life of purpose and value, even if it means dedicating more time to work than relaxation, but that's just me. Then again, in 25 years I may feel different!

I simply don't place the same worth or the same purpose on every aspect of my life. There are things I love more than others, things I don't mind dedicating extra time to. And if you talk to any successful person, they'll tell you that balance is only part of the equation.

These days everybody likes to talk about "work-life balance," but many of the folks who really get stuff done simply don't lead balanced lives. In fact, some career coaches believe you *can't* be ultra-successful at your calling or vocation if you try to balance everything in your life.

What I have learned is that it's not about balance— it's about harmonizing the dissonance in your life.

We live in a cacophonous world. Notes of discord and disagreement surround us all. From the deafening deluge of social media we see every day to our soul-sucking consumer culture to the demands in our professional lives and the difficulties in our private ones, we are constantly bombarded by mental and spiritual noise. This can reach an ear-splitting pitch if we allow it.

The challenge, then, is to eliminate the frequencies that are causing the most discordant notes in your life, be they people, places, or things. In life, as in music, you don't need to play all the notes all the time. You just need the right notes.

I am careful to only engage in activities, associate with people, embrace issues, take on assignments, and make commitments that can coexist harmoniously with what I have set out to achieve in my life.

You can spot the dissonant notes in your life pretty easily. They want you to major in the minors. They want you to fit in, not stand out. They diminish your possibilities. They try to buy your soul at a discount.

When you start to hear noise that interferes with the way you want to live your life, you've got to put it on mute. Ask yourself, "Is this enriching me?" If the answer is no, then tune it out. Otherwise it will do all it can to silence the exuberant music in your life.

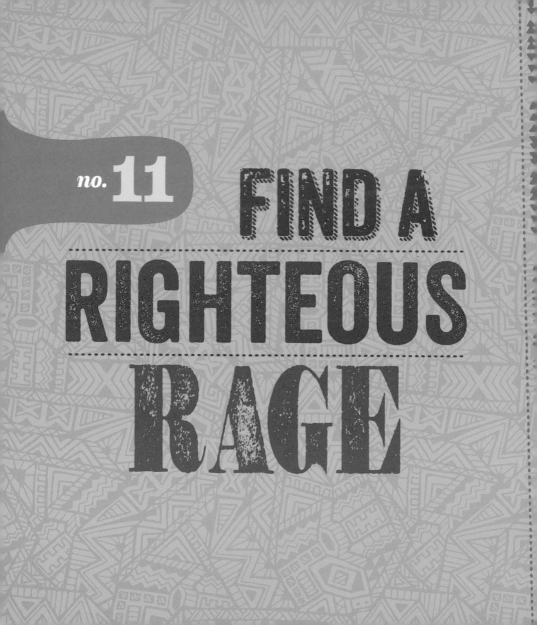

no. **11**

FIND A RIGHTEOUS RAGE

RAGE *isn't hard to find in America.*

Just take a trip on the freeways near my home in Los Angeles and you'll see road rage everywhere. People getting cut off by other cars. Folks not having the common courtesy to wave thanks when someone in the next lane lets them merge or turn. And let's not even get started on how a three-mile drive can take an hour or more.

This sort of rage comes from low-level outside influences we feel being directed at us. But there's a different kind of rage that we don't see enough of in America today: righteous rage.

We are all human beings, but we don't come into the fullness of our own *humanity* until we learn to be concerned about the well-being of others. If you cannot have empathy—which is different from sympathy—for others, if you don't consider others to be significant, how much benevolence can you really have inside?

I have learned that before you can fulfill your potential, you must develop a sense of outrage—a righteous rage. There are so many different things wrong with our world that there must be something that burdens your soul, makes your heart heavy. Let it push you to become an agitator who will do something about a particular injustice, evil, or inequity.

For me, it started September 12th, 1983, when my friend Denver Smith, star of our Indiana University football team, was killed by White police officers. That atrocity ignited a fire of righteous rage that burns in my heart to this day; it lights the path of service and social justice I've sought to stay on ever since. My focus has moved from issue to issue over time, but the commitment will always stay the same.

It comes down to what the great Dr. Martin Luther King, Jr., called the most persistent and urgent question we all face: What are we doing for others?

When we see anyone else's humanity being contested, it should spur us to act. We all have a soul; yours should be vexed by the inhumane treatment you see happening around you. Witnessing an injustice should make you feel a little dirty, make you feel a little uncomfortable, unsettled, your spiritual foundation unhinged.

That cause will be different for each of us. Maybe animal rights stir a passion inside you. Maybe it's combating racism, whether on the streets of Ferguson, Missouri, or in your local town. Maybe it's reversing the tide of environmental degradation happening at home and throughout the world.

Whatever it is, it's crucial to let your natural empathy move you.

The reality is that most of us are aware of injustices that happen all the time, but we do nothing about them. Eventually we have to stop simply looking and begin to really *see*, to move from inactive to proactive.

I counsel many young people as part of my ongoing social entrepreneurial work. I know when I see a young person who gets it—who cares about the condition and suffering of the world—and I can see a clear image of where that life is

headed. These fortunate young people have taken a big step at an early age toward becoming fully human, toward reaching fundamental maturity. By contrast, I've noticed that people who take longer to find their spark of motivation may not face such positive futures.

Finding your passionate indignation changes your spiritual and social DNA permanently. The sooner you find the flicker that lights the fire of righteous rage in your soul, the brighter you'll burn

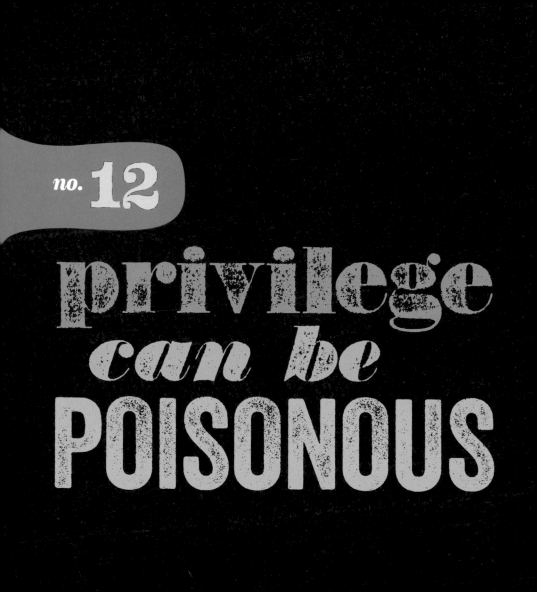

no. 12

privilege
can be
POISONOUS

AS A poor child

growing up in a family of 13 people in a three-bedroom, one-bath trailer, I spent my Saturday mornings watching the Jackson 5 on TV and fantasizing about what it would be like to be Michael Jackson, to have that famous last name.

The other kids made fun of my name, as kids will do, calling me "Travis Smelly" to be mean. *But if I was called Michael Jackson*, I thought, *imagine how different my life would be!*

Now I have a much better idea of exactly how different.

When I was young, I was turned on by the idea of being a person of privilege. It wasn't so much about the riches or the fame, but the opportunities that privilege could provide. I wanted a launching pad, a foundation to help me get into the stratosphere, to do whatever I wanted to do.

The older I got, the harder I worked. The more I accomplished, the more I realized that there is a sublime joy, a peace, and indeed a beauty in being able to get lift-off on your own. Not that any one of us makes this journey solo; we all need help from supporters and collaborators. I am not self-made, as some people occasionally describe me. I am, in fact, social-made.

Now that I'm older, I've met many folks whose last names and legacies are attached to them like heavy anchors they must carry around their whole lives. I have come to appreciate that privilege can actually be poisonous.

I think of former Illinois congressman Jesse Jackson, Jr., who told me before his legal troubles began, "You have no idea how much I get judged because of who my father is." If you look at his voting record on the hill, you'll see that the brother never missed a vote—he was too worried he'd be criticized for being a fly-by-night, parachuting-in politician. Just as his father was criticized for carrying on his social justice work.

Imagine what that patrilineal pressure did to Paul Robeson, Jr., son of the brilliant singer and actor; or Martin Luther King III, son of Dr. King, Jr. Even Max Brooks, whose father is the comedic genius Mel, has admitted he still struggles to make a name of his own—despite his success as a writer.

Most of us are not people of privilege so don't get caught hating on somebody else's game, wishing you had that launching pad, or a certain last name, or the kind of economic means that privilege can provide.

Whatever your assignment is in the world—whatever gift, talent, skill, vocation, or purpose you have—know that you were born with enough innate, requisite ability and ambition to get the job done.

The challenge is figuring out what that vocation is, nurturing those gifts, becoming an expert at what you do. That's hard enough in life. Don't waste energy craving what others have. If you're not careful, craving becomes coveting. Don't risk missing the chance to be the best and the most privileged *you* possible.

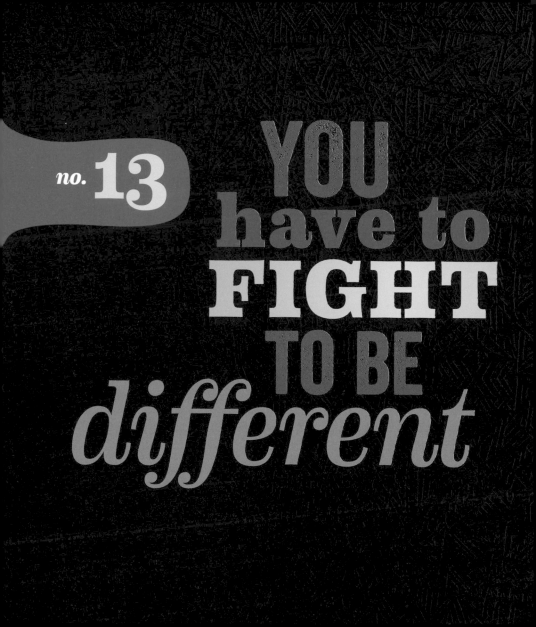

no. **13**

YOU
have to
FIGHT
TO BE
different

i came into my own

as an African American broadcaster in an African American media environment, first on Black radio in Los Angeles, then nationally on the *Tom Joyner Morning Show,* and then with my own nightly talk show on the Black Entertainment Television network. I was lucky enough to get to hone my craft while being nurtured in a Black space—a beautiful thing.

After being let go by BET, I eventually found myself transitioning into a new situation that was literally a contrast in Black and White. I went to work for National Public Radio. When I arrived, there were those who doubted I would last.

I received letters from listeners telling me I laughed too boisterously. That I talked too loud. That I spoke too fast. That I needed to dial back my energy. That my diction wasn't as good as others'—although nobody accused me of splitting infinitives or leaving participles dangling.

Let's face it: NPR is not a Black person's medium per se. I was the first to push into that space, and my style was in high contrast to the standard "public radio voice" and demeanor—a calm and cool manner of expression listeners had grown accustomed to.

I remember telling myself that if I was going to make it at NPR—and, later, on PBS, the Public Broadcasting Service—I was going to make it by embracing my authentic self. I was not going to obscure who I really was.

I've learned that being your authentic self can, at times, be incredibly inconvenient. It can run counter to an environment that you're trying to break into or a culture at a workplace where you're trying to get a job. It might make you stand out like a sore thumb among your friends and peers, or confound what everybody else in a room thinks about an idea or innovation.

But it's crucial you believe in who you are.

You must be willing to be your authentic self—fly or fail.

I've seen so many people subvert their real selves to try to please others or fit in. I'm particularly conscious of this on the racial front, having watched Black people cross over into a White environment because they think they have to deny who they really are to be successful.

I've also seen this with respect to religion, to ideology, to political beliefs—in every area of human engagement, in fact. People think they have to obscure their true selves in order to be accepted, to succeed in a given environment.

At NPR, I had a realization: If they'd wanted the same old tried-and-true radio personality, there was a deep reservoir of people they could have tapped into.

But they didn't want that. They wanted *me*. So why should I go in there and try to be something I'm not?

I've also come to realize that people who try to obscure their authentic selves fail at a far greater rate than those who embrace who they fundamentally are. The reason? It's just not sustainable. Eventually people are going to see through you, and then the frauds get caught.

The only vocation in life where people find true joy in being somebody else is acting. So if you're not a thespian and you're trying to act like somebody else every day, you're out of character and will never get the part.

no. **14**

MORE FORCE CAN MEAN LESS EFFECT

During the writing of this book,

Israel and Palestine were going at it again. The Israelis invaded the Gaza Strip to stop militants from firing rockets into Israel. A peaceful juncture arrived only when Israel began to catch hell and received pushback for its excessive use of force. Even the United States called their actions disgraceful—and we're their biggest allies in the world.

Let me be clear: I'm not about to get into the politics of the Middle East here. If the two sides haven't been able to solve their conflict after thousands of years, I definitely can't solve it in a 500-word essay.

The point, rather, is to note that sometimes the more force you apply, the less effective it becomes. This is as true for Israel as it is for Tavis Smiley and everyone else.

I've learned this lesson many times over in my capacity as an entrepreneur, as the leader of a company, as a content creator—in all these various roles.

When you're driven, you tend to want to drive other people too.

You don't mean any harm; you just want to get the work done. But over the years I've learned that sometimes I need to pump the brakes.

This lesson applies to all aspects of my life. With my staff, especially the young folks I love to hire and watch grow. It's there at the negotiating table when I'm trying to get a deal done. I apply it to relationships when I'm trying to persuade another person to see it my way. And I'm mindful of it with an audience, in my efforts to convince a crowd that there's value in how I think about a particular issue.

You can learn what amount of force is appropriate in any given situation only by trial and error—and it may take you the rest of your life to figure it out. I have had my share of moments when I kept pushing long past the point of effectiveness. It's happened in personal connections. Women I've dated have later come back and told me, "Tavis, you're great. But when I came to you with a really sensitive concern, you only had one emotional gear. Sometimes all I needed was a hug or a kind word, not another lecture on how things ought to be handled."

I've experienced it in business too. It's often said that in business you don't get what you deserve: you get what you negotiate. I've absolutely been at the bargaining table when, because I believed I had to win every point, I ended up losing the whole deal.

When his band was trying to force a groove or was overplaying a section, the late, great Michael Jackson would tell them, "You got to let it simmer." In life, sometimes you've got to let things quiet down, let them marinate in reason and introspection. If you don't, you could easily lose the girl or the guy or the deal, or the team at work might not achieve what you're trying to accomplish. Not every situation requires you to act like a pile driver. Knowing the right amount of force to apply will go far in keeping your approach balanced and your goals on track.

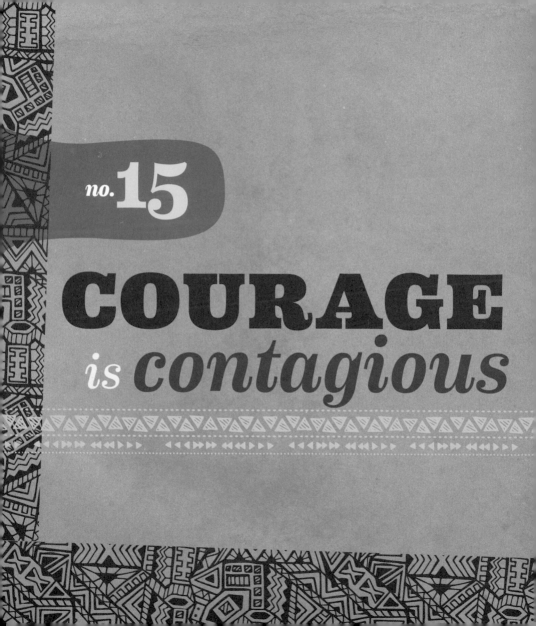

no.**15**

COURAGE
is contagious

the great Maya Angelou

—my friend and surrogate mother for 28 years—used to engage in the same debate with me over and over again. We'd been doing it for longer than I can remember. To be fair, she mostly had me from the start, but it was a beautiful thing to engage with that mind.

She would ask me which virtue I believed was the greatest.

My answer was love. The Bible says that of faith, hope, and love, the greatest is love.

Then I asked her what she thought the greatest virtue was.

"Courage," she said, "because it takes courage to love."

Hard to argue with that.

And yet today people seem crippled in their ability to be courageous, to risk anything that doesn't involve some potential for self-aggrandizement: more money, more cars, more fame.

Courage is terribly uncommon.

This confounds me, because the people we respect and admire most are always the ones who are willing to act courageously. The lesson I've learned from studying and watching the lives of those noble risk-takers is that courage is contagious. It inspires others. It emboldens others. It makes what seemed impossible possible.

Each of us, in our lives, has to find a way to build courage—the key word here being *build*.

Dr. Angelou instructed us all to practice courage. It begins in small ways, in small settings, in small acts. You start building it by discouraging insensitive and degrading comments among friends. It grows when you defend someone against others when it's not the convenient thing to do. It grows more when you make the right choice even when no one else is around to give you credit.

At first you practice courage in small stages, in baby steps. You have to exercise courage like a muscle. It will take time and effort to get it into shape. But it's essential that all of us do this, because at some point we will all be called upon to act fearlessly.

If you haven't started to practice, when that moment of truth comes and you're put on the spot and courage is demanded of you, will you act courageously? Or will you act with cowardice?

If you haven't been working on it, if your courage has atrophied or gone slack, how will you find the strength to do what's right?

The courage question *will* come up—remember, in life some years ask questions. Usually it isn't really a case of needing to be Wonder Woman or Superman—even if that's what it feels like at the time—and it can happen anywhere: in the workplace, in a relationship, in a familial setting, in public. But it takes conditioning to ensure that when the moment arrives, you'll be in the best shape possible to take it on.

Know that what might at first feel burdensome will serve as inspiration for others to start their own program of courage conditioning.

no. 16

YOU
HAVE
THE
RIGHT
to
REMAIN
SILENT

We're all familiar with the Miranda rights

that the police are required to read to you if, God forbid, you've been arrested. The first one is "You have the right to remain silent."

What too many people don't understand is that each of us can exercise that right every day, all the time. Sometimes, the best thing you can do is just keep quiet.

We live in a world where everyone's talking but very few people communicate much of substance. James Brown described it in his song "Talkin' Loud and Sayin' Nothing." We all know that the global temperature is on the rise. Some of that is due to global warming. But maybe some of it is all the hot air in this country.

By nature and occupation, I am a talker. I enjoy having my say. For the longest time, I would never dream of conceding an argument. I'd fight for my opinion until my lungs gave out.

But now I've learned that I *don't* have to have the last word—and sometimes I don't even have to have the first! I used to go into meetings and feel compelled to get all my stuff out there before anybody else could speak. I know better now. If it's not my discussion to lead, then it's better to sit and listen, especially in a business negotiation. I've learned to wait and see what someone else puts on the table first; sometimes it has turned out that the deal they offered me was better than what I would have asked for, or what I thought I was going to get.

But the benefits of exercising your right to remain silent go beyond business dealings. There's a profundity, a brilliance, a beauty in the strategy of embracing the quiet. When you're silent, you can keep others guessing. People often assume there is something implicit in what you leave unsaid—and that can be very powerful.

When the Monica Lewinsky circus was at its peak, news crews used to park in front of the house of Vernon Jordan, a close aide to President Clinton. And every morning Vernon would exit his house, dapper as always, smile to the news crews, say "Good morning," and walk to his car.

"Good morning." That's all he ever said.

For Vernon, the simple presence of cameras and microphones didn't make him feel compelled to say anything. Too often we think that just because everyone else is talking, we have to join the chatter.

Just because people ask you questions doesn't mean you have to answer them. Especially not on their terms.

Are the questions biased, leading, or unfair? You don't have to answer them. Did you get pulled into a conversation you don't want to be in? You can simply stop participating. Sometimes what you don't say can be the most important contribution you make to a situation.

My grandmother would always tell me, "Baby, the truth don't move." Sometimes the wisest thing you can do is let the truth stand for itself—and not try to prop it up with your own words.

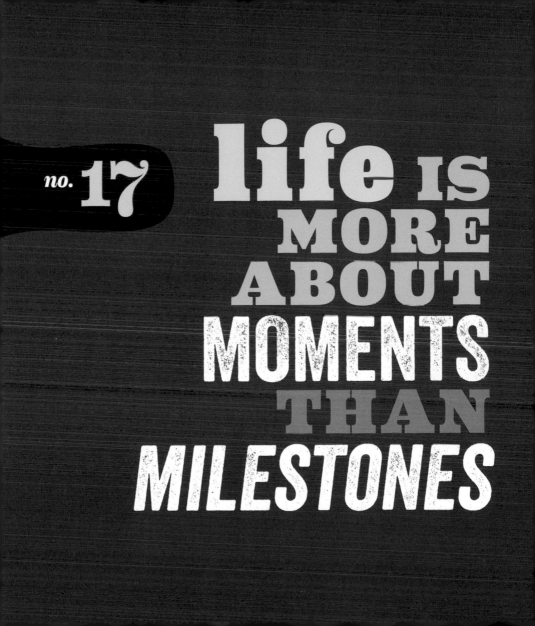

no. 17

life IS MORE ABOUT MOMENTS THAN MILESTONES

We are conditioned *from birth* to chase milestones.

It begins when everyone makes a fuss over our first birthday. Next, we're turning five—time for kindergarten. Then we reach double digits. Shortly after, we become teenagers. Then it's 16—a driver's license. Next, we're 18—graduating high school and off to college. After all that, we're 21—finally able to drink legally!

Somewhere down the road, after all the hustle to go to the right school, get the right degree, find the right job, buy the right house in the right part of town, have the right friends and the right clothes and the right car, somewhere along the way and unfortunately too late for some of us, we realize that life is far more about moments than it is about milestones.

There's a reason why we call them "milestones"—not "feet-stones" or "yard-stones."

It's because we have to travel a good distance to reach them. But if you focus solely on the milestones, think of all you're missing in between.

I'm as guilty as anyone; I admit it. I've been chasing milestones. I'm not a workaholic, but I am driven. I'm driven to chase the next big thing. I want to leave the world a better place when I depart than it was when I arrived. I want to make some meaningful and significant contributions, and I don't apologize for saying that, if successful, I'd like to be acknowledged at some point for what I've attempted to do for humankind.

But I am at the point now in my life where I've learned that if all you're doing is chasing milestones, you miss out on the opportunities to create memories. Then the milestones end up feeling a little underwhelming once you get there to celebrate them. They're not as exciting; they're not as rewarding.

I don't have a wife or children yet, and I think about that sometimes: Who do I have to share these milestones with? Who will I grow old with?

My friends will tell you that I'm the most loyal person they know, but I frequently don't take the simple, very important step needed to keep friendships going. Specifically, I'm not the guy that picks up the phone to call people as often as I should.

I'm not the most nurturing guy. I've become aware that I need to start working on that, because encouraging and caring for one another is a basic step toward creating meaningful moments.

I'm the only member of my family living in Los Angeles. I have 9 brothers and sisters, and I now have 31 nieces and nephews. I can't even remember all their names! Cut me some slack now—31 is *a lot*!

I want to own the fact that I just don't get back to Indiana often enough. I should spend more time with my family. My mother complains that I don't show up to all the family reunions, and she's right to do so. I'm taking this lesson more seriously the older I get. We all should. Make time for the memories, because they're what matter most in the end.

no. **18**

sometimes
YOUR
VULNERABILITIES
will *outnumber*
your
POSSIBILITIES

the *Children's* Defense Fund

promotes some of its work with a simple prayer that I find very powerful: "Lord, be good to me. The sea is so wide, and my boat is so small."

I believe the meaning of the prayer is one that all Americans—regardless of their faith—can understand today.

I once gave a graduation speech at Drexel University in Pennsylvania and posed this question to the audience: How do we create lives of meaning and value in a world where, for many of us, our vulnerabilities outnumber our possibilities?

Vulnerabilities are all around us. In July 2014, a poll conducted by Rasmussen Reports showed that 52 percent of Americans believe our country's best days are behind us. We collectively quake over concerns about our fragile economy, stagnant wages, CEOs getting rich at home while shipping jobs abroad, persistent income inequality, the dearth of jobs for young college graduates, the fact that education—for Black Americans *or* White Americans—isn't the great economic equalizer it once was, how crime has crippled many communities, the toll of endless wars around the globe. I could go on and on.

Americans are feeling **vulnerable** in ways they haven't for generations.

In that auditorium at Drexel, I looked out over the sea of soon-to-be-graduates and their families, friends, and well-wishers. I ventured to guess that a lot of people in that audience had done everything "right," yet they were sitting there unemployed, with their retirement funds gone, on the verge of losing their homes.

Too many in the audience sadly and knowingly nodded their heads as I spoke.

So what do we do when all these vulnerabilities in our lives outnumber the potential for good we hoped to realize? As I've said before, there is a storm brewing out at sea in each of our lives. We don't know when it's coming, but it is impending. Each of us has to prepare for that storm.

Start by analyzing what you place value on. Too many of us plant undeserving value on material possessions. Instead, bank on experiences and relationships and virtues—these weather any storm and matter the most to our souls. Believe it or not, the world doesn't revolve around you. There are a lot of other folks in that orbit who need what you can bring them. Prepare your soul now so when that storm hits your own life, you'll be capable instead of vulnerable.

An anchor can keep us from being swept away by the waves that threaten to drown us. Ground yourself in something greater than you and that fills you with hope. The little prayer I mentioned above means so much to me. As a person of faith, I believe in a higher power; I can place my faith and hope in that when the sea seems so wide and my boat so small.

It's also important to remember that there's a difference between optimism and belief, hope, and faith.

Optimism suggests that there is a set of facts, circumstances, or conditions—something you can see,

feel, or touch—that gives you reason to believe that things are going to get better.

When things are cruising along and times are good, that's usually enough for folks. But when those challenging vulnerabilities begin to mount, and possibilities seem to diminish, optimism alone is no match for what you have to deal with. People, places, and things simply don't hold up—a spiritual response is what's required. A belief system.

Hope and faith are fundamentally different things.

Hope means that, in spite of all the evidence to the contrary, you have faith that things are going to work out. Hope helps to anchor you as a storm rages around you—you have faith the sun will be back again one day. It's hope that keeps misery from having the last word.

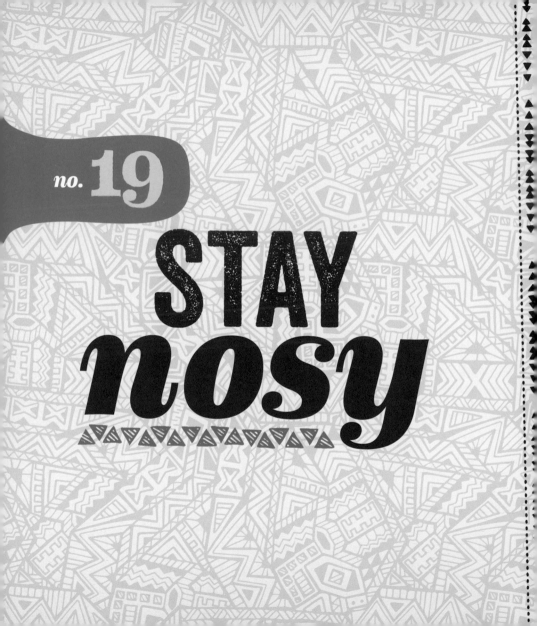

no. **19**

STAY
nosy

When I was a *little boy,*

my grandmother Big Mama used to say to me all the time, "Tavis, there are twenty-four hours in the day. Twelve hours to mind your business, and twelve hours to leave other folks' business alone."

In other words: Stop being nosy! My grandmother couldn't stand people who were up in everybody else's business all the time.

I get what Big Mama meant, and she was right—then. But these days we live in a world where everybody has access to what used to be confidential personal information. Our culture has blurred the boundary between the private and the public. Without giving it a thought, people freely put their personal business on display, right out in the open. On Facebook and Twitter and YouTube and Instagram, through texting and e-mails and videos. Everything is out there—and it's everywhere.

As a child, I took Big Mama's advice and kept to myself. But I've learned throughout my life that you should, in fact, stay nosy. By that I mean you have to stay inquisitive. You have to go on being curious. Information has never been easier to come by.

So I say stick your nose where it doesn't belong. Because how else can you sniff out what the possibilities are or where the dangers lie?

I'm a curious person. That's what makes my TV and radio shows work. I've found that most successful people are also curious. For example, I read a lot about and talk to CEOs of big companies, and the one thing they all have in common is that they ask a lot of questions. They're inquisitive. People think CEOs are the ones who already know everything, but they're really just the people most interested in continuing to learn all they can to make the best business decisions possible.

CEOs aren't the only ones who carry the curiosity gene, though.

I remember when I was first trying to get the legendary musician Prince on my TV show. We finally connected, and he invited me to lunch. A meeting that was supposed to last an hour turned into a four-hour conversation.

I left the restaurant thinking: *I got him! He's going to come on my show!*

Ultimately he did—and has appeared on it many times since. But I misread that initial meeting. Later, I realized that we'd spent almost the entire time talking about *me*. Prince had flipped the script; he had been the one doing the interviewing that day! He was curious about me and what my story was, and wanted to get to know me before he was willing to come on the show.

Another righteously nosy person was diplomat Richard Holbrooke. He was the go-to international statesman for every Democratic president from Jimmy Carter on. Holbrooke had been our ambassador to the United Nations, helping bring peace to warring countries.

I finally got Holbrooke on the show, via satellite between New York City and Los Angeles. Now, these feeds are very expensive. Once we had him on the line, Holbrooke would not let me start the interview because of all the questions he wanted to ask me—he was so curious. I couldn't say what I was thinking out loud because it was, after all, Richard Holbrooke, but this thought kept running through my head: *Dude, you're eating up my satellite time! Can you just let me do my job?*

Because I hadn't interviewed him before, he wanted to know just who it was he was talking to. That curiosity, that desire to know more—and an ability to ask endless on-point questions—was a great asset for a person who regularly walked into tense negotiating situations. Holbrooke needed to know everything he could about the topic at hand before those talks began so he could achieve his goal. He was successful almost every time.

Too often today we deal in monologue; there's very little dialogue. People aren't as curious about the world as they should be. There's so much potential for enlightenment out there at our disposal—we can read, watch, or hear something on any topic with a few clicks. But information doesn't equal insight, and knowledge isn't the same thing as wisdom. Staying nosy and indulging curiosity are crucial to bridging those gaps.

BE *humble* with your **CREATIVITY** **AND** *gracious* with your **SUCCESS**

I've traveled the world *and beyond* with Quincy Jones.

That's a bit of an exaggeration. I was firmly planted in my studio in Los Angeles, but Q and I were talking to the astronauts who were in outer space on the space shuttle *Atlantis*. They'd just been woken up to Q's recording of "Fly Me to the Moon" with Frank Sinatra, and we got to speak to them by satellite. This remains one of the highlights of my broadcasting career.

Q is truly a renaissance man. He's been a part of everything, from music to film to politics to philanthropy. When you're with Q, you're going to have a good time—and you'll be treated like royalty, because that's how Q operates.

Not too long ago, we happened to be seated next to each other on a flight to Boston. We were headed to the same event—a conference on social entrepreneurship—and I had the privilege of getting to talk his ear off the whole flight.

Right before we landed I asked him, "What would you say is the most important lesson you've learned after all the success that you've had?"

He thought for just a moment and then replied, "You've got to be humble with your creativity and gracious with your success."

I thought, *What a powerful insight!* In some ways, it's also a wonderful definition of greatness.

I've discovered that too few people even think to use the words *humble* and *gracious* anymore. Too few people who are creative and successful practice the sort of greatness Q described.

But each and every one of us can work on being great by taking Q's words to heart. You don't even need to be a creative person for this to apply to your life. Whatever your vocation is, whatever your calling, be humble in the pursuit of it. When you succeed, be gracious about what you have accomplished.

I was once honored to host a discussion with the brilliant composers and conductors John Williams, Gustavo Santaolalla, and Gustavo Dudamel. I was waiting backstage for Williams to arrive. He is, of course, a legend. Steven Spielberg's musical muse, the genius behind the music for so many films, including *Star Wars*. He's an Academy Award–nominated composer dozens of times over.

When he saw me he said, "Tavis Smiley, I'm so honored to see you again. I just said to someone earlier today, 'I wonder if Tavis will remember meeting me on his show.'"

Me remember meeting *him*?! I said, "Of *course* I remember having you on." But then I thought, *What a humble cat.*

The truth is that humility and humbleness, gratitude and graciousness, win every time. There are so few things in life that we can point to as constants—but these traits never fail to impress.

These virtues are so deeply rooted in goodness that it's strange those of us striving to be winners don't embrace them more often. In an ideal world, humility and graciousness would spring forth from us naturally, and without hesitation.

SPEND TIME *in* STILLNESS

After the tragic death of the legendary performer Michael Jackson,

the public learned of the deep, troubling struggle he had with resting his body and mind. His fierce mental drive never allowed him to take a break, even for a moment.

Once, when a member of his concert crew suggested that he get some sleep after endless nights of nonstop work, Michael resisted.

"You don't understand," he said. "If I'm not there to receive the ideas, God might give them to Prince."

Michael said this earnestly, without a trace of humor.

Being driven and passionate are absolutely critical ingredients to success. But left unchecked and unexamined, the pull to always be "on" can make you burn out, just like a lightbulb. It's critical to spend part of your day in stillness, to take some quiet time to just stop and think. Do this on a regular basis.

For many years, I, too, had the mind-set that if I slowed down, if I pulled over, if I stopped for even a second, the competition would catch up to me. Or I'd lose out on the big interview. Or I'd miss an opportunity that I'd never get back.

However, two truths about this are now permanent fixtures in my head.

First, if you're succeeding at being the best you can be, demonstrating your highest level of excellence, you simply become irreplaceable. I frequently have to turn down invitations to events because of my busy schedule and multiple commitments. What I eventually figured out is that, when they can't book me, they try to find somebody "like Tavis." But there is only one me. Any replacement will fall at least a little short of the genuine article.

Second, stillness has tremendous value. Stepping back and practicing introspection and reflection should be a priority of the highest order. Some of my best ideas and epiphanies have come during quiet moments, when I disengage from the chatter and demands of life and just be still.

When you're "on" all the time, your mind is able to process only what it is you're feverishly focusing on.

You end up missing details, overlooking life's subtleties, bypassing specifics. You lose track of the small stuff. Sometimes, the most important occurrences on any given day are simple things.

The universe often speaks to us in a still, small voice. Whatever it's trying to say can too easily be drowned out by the roar of constant noise that comes with going full force all day, every day. You can't afford to miss those messages. But there's good news: During the quiet moments they will try again to make themselves known to you. Be sure to make time to be still if only for a few minutes a day.

no. 22 SOMETIMES *good-bye* is a GIFT

It's a simple truth that in life

you're going to hear "good-bye" many times. From employers. From family members. From someone you're in a relationship with. In all sorts of situations, opportunities, and interactions, either you or the person you're involved with will be shown the door.

Let's be clear: It doesn't feel good. Not the first time, not the next time, and not the last time. It *never* feels good. This is one of those perennial lessons that is best learned early on. No one gets let go from a job or a relationship and feels good about it. Even if you hated the job, wanted out, and you talked about quitting a thousand times, nobody likes being told, "You're fired." Regardless of the context or the reason, people don't want to have that Donald Trump moment!

But sometimes good-bye is a gift. In the moment you don't realize it, you can't see it, you don't understand the reason why it happened. But looking at it in retrospect sometime later, it dawns on you: "Man, that good-bye was a blessing!"

I think back to my unsuccessful run for the Los Angeles City Council in 1987. Initially I was crushed by losing. But in the end, the voters did me a favor. If I'd been elected, I might still be signing off on pothole repairs and not doing the work I was called to do.

Then there was the time I lost my job at BET, through no fault of my own. Business is business, as they say, and I got stuck with a pink slip. But if I hadn't been shown the door at BET, I might never have gone on to do public television and radio work. I may have remained a household name in Black America only.

The truly difficult good-byes are between you and loved ones. The memories that we accumulate, especially those created within relationships, are what truly constitute life.

There's an old adage that says people come into your life for a reason, a season, or a lifetime.

I heard this years ago, and back then it sounded to me like a platitude. But now, it sounds like real wisdom. What we don't grasp until later in life is that most of those people settle into the first two categories.

When people enter into your life for a reason, identify that reason, learn from that reason, and be made better by it. When it's just for a season, revel in the splendor of that season, soak up all you can, but when fall turns to winter, accept that it's time to say good-bye. And be thankful when you're blessed by the rare lifelong relationship that comes along.

If you don't have perspective, when you get to the point where the person who's there for a reason or a season comes and goes—either because they jumped or you pushed them away—if you're naive about how this process works, you'll be devastated.

Make it a point to try to understand why it was time to say good-bye, embrace what good came from it, and compartmentalize what feelings you have about the experience so you can handle the day-to-day situations that follow. Then it's time to move on.

no. 23 your
work
becomes
your
AFTERLIFE

Isn't it rare for somebody to turn out to be exactly who you thought he or she was?

My friend Jance happened to be one of those rare, beautiful people.

On the surface, Jance was an ordinary person. He sold shoes at Neiman Marcus in Beverly Hills. Everybody loved him. He was sharp, amiable, warm, stylish, crisply dressed, and decent. He knew exactly how to make you look your best.

Everybody loved Jance.

Jance and his family eventually moved back home to Cleveland, Ohio, where his wife was from. He had a number of kids, including a little girl with special needs, and they required more help than they were getting in California.

One night, their split-level house caught fire. Everybody was asleep upstairs when it started, but Jance was able to wake them. He got them all to a second-floor balcony and made each one jump to the ground below. His wife went first. She broke her leg when she landed, but still managed to cushion the falls of the children who came after.

After they were safely on the ground below, Jance told each one of them how much he loved them, then he headed back inside. You see, his special-needs daughter was still in there, and he had to try to save her.

When the firefighters found their remains, Jance was on his knees, overcome by the heat and the smoke, still holding his daughter in his arms. Even if it meant sacrificing his own life, he would not leave her alone in that burning house.

When I heard the news, tears quickly welled up in my eyes, of course, but I also couldn't help smiling—that was Jance! Even in his final moments, he was exactly the person I thought he was. People kept calling him a hero, but I knew that it was both simpler and more profound: That was simply Jance. You had better believe people would remember him more for his final sacrifice than for how many pairs of shoes he sold.

Long after you're gone, the impact you've had on people—in Jance's case, the love, the service, the reveling in the humanity of others—will be what lives on. Life is not just about accomplishments, but also about contributions. As I've said before, it's more about the intimate moments than the milestones.

> **The older I get, the more I've come to realize that the work you do becomes your afterlife.**

As I chronicled in my book *Fail Up*, I approached the age of 40 terrified that I would not accomplish everything I wanted to before I died. I don't fear that anymore, though, because I simply realize that I *won't* get it all done. My concern now is more about how well I'll succeed at the things I *am* able to accomplish.

Why are we still talking about Abraham Lincoln, Dr. King, Mother Teresa, and Nelson Mandela long after they're gone? It's because the great work they did with people became their afterlife. Our contributions in life don't stop when we do. We have the chance to write our own eulogies, and then to go out and live them. We simply have to decide what impression we want to leave on the world during our lifetimes and how we want to be judged when we're gone.

The people who understand this live life in unique ways. They make decisions and choices different from the average person's. Their priorities are selfless, and they're always more concerned about loved ones than about themselves.

To this day, we're still talking about Jance. There are people like him you've never heard of all over the world, but you can be sure others will continue to talk about them because the lives they led touched people. And all the people whose lives were touched feel blessed to have known them. Wouldn't we all like to know that, one day, someone will say with a knowing smile that we were exactly who they thought we were?

no. **24**

fall *in* LOVE

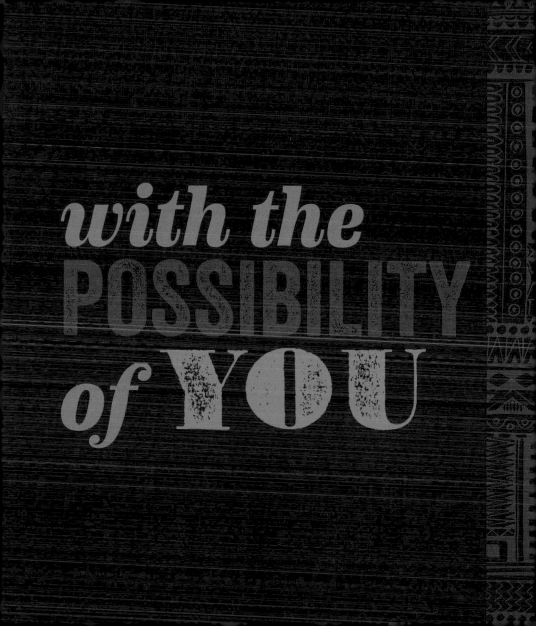

with the **POSSIBILITY** *of* **YOU**

Have you ever met people who you want more for than they seem to want for *themselves*?

You can see their gifts, you can see their potential, you can see their talents, but *they* have yet to fall in love with the possibility of who they could be, or what they could achieve.

For a society hooked on looking at itself in selfies, on Facebook, and in the mirror, it is just amazing what we don't see.

I encounter so many people who, for a variety of reasons, simply don't like themselves. I can tell by their body language when I walk up to them. I can hear it in their voices when we speak. I watch how they interact with others, and it's so apparent. Too many people are not in love with the possibility of what and who they can become. This is especially the case among young people, and it breaks my heart.

We live in a world where people want to be everything except who they already are. In some ways this helps explain the multibillion-dollar fashion, makeup, cosmetic surgery, diet, and workout-fad industries. They're catering to a culture of people obsessed with transforming themselves into someone or something else.

Just as some people self-medicate through one addiction or another, others self-fabricate new identities as a way to avoid dealing with the reality of who they really are. Some of this springs from the dissatisfaction people have with their physique and/or phenotype—with their physical selves. But really, most of what lies at the core of our inability to fall in love with who we are and who we could possibly become is buried in our inner lives, our belief systems, and false ideas that society pounds into us.

Too many people live with a lack of self-confidence, self-determination, and self-awareness. So much of what keeps people from discovering wiser motivations and empowerments is the intimidation they experience at the hands of others. They've allowed themselves to be bullied. Out of who they are. Out of what they could be. People demonize or diminish us, let us know they have only low expectations of us, or force us into an environment starved of the nutrients our souls and spirits need.

We've been Jedi mind-tricked into not believing in or recognizing our own possibilities.

Maya Angelou liked to paraphrase Terence, a Roman playwright of North African descent: "We are all human; therefore, nothing human can be alien to us." To discover your true potential, it's important to believe this. Let nothing be alien to you; let nothing intimidate you. There's nothing that should ever hold you back from trying your hand at . . . anything.

Life presents us with an enormous range of possibilities. Unless you try, you will never know what you're capable of.

Only by leaving our comfort zones do we begin to discover the reservoirs of potential that reside in each of us. No effort is a waste of time. All it takes is the courage to love the possibility of you.

no. **25**

TO love IS TO SUFFER

When we think of love, we think of joy, of contentment, of passion, of hope, and of beauty.

When we think of love, we never think of suffering— but to love is to suffer.

When you love people—when you love humanity—you suffer because you feel their pain. Which is to say you empathize: You identify with and share the feelings of the one suffering. This is a far deeper response than sympathy, which isn't much more than pity and consolation. Sometimes trying to help someone will hurt you, especially when that person doesn't want your help. Sometimes people choose to accept their suffering rather than have it healed. Your love is then rejected, which doesn't feel good.

For me the greatest example of this lesson is Jesus. As a person of faith, I recognize His decision to go to the cross to suffer for our sins as the ultimate sacrifice for humanity.

People suffer for the individuals they love as well. When my family moved from Mississippi to Indiana, it caused my mother tremendous pain. She hated it there, but my father's job was transferred and she loved him, so the family went. Only years later did she tell me how she cried every day after my father left for work. Now, of course, Indiana's become her home. But her love for her husband and her family initially caused her to suffer for them.

In big and small ways, for significant things and those of little importance, on every level, love can cause suffering.

And let's be clear: It works both ways. Eventually you're going to make somebody suffer too!

The Bible tells us to love our enemies—the people who have the most interest in hurting us. It also tells us to love our neighbors. That can be mighty difficult, whether your neighbors next door have a yapping dog and play loud music, or live on the opposite side of the Palestinian-Israeli border.

Loving people is the most difficult thing to do. It means having to accept suffering and learning to forgive.

As I noted in my book *Death of a King*, Dr. Martin Luther King, Jr., had his phone and home wiretapped for years by the FBI. Yet, even during those darkest days, when seemingly everyone had turned against him, Dr. King was never once heard on tape contesting the humanity of others. Imagine that: being who you truly are, when no one is around to listen, behind closed doors. He had accepted that he would suffer for loving humanity—and he had learned to forgive his enemies.

This is not a lesson with a solution. Love isn't an either/or equation. Love is both/and. It holds all the good stuff—the joy, contentment, passion, hope, and beauty—and is responsible for all the suffering as well. You can't compartmentalize love. It is a total, uncompromising package. There are some things in life that we must simply learn to accept, and the duality of love is one of them.

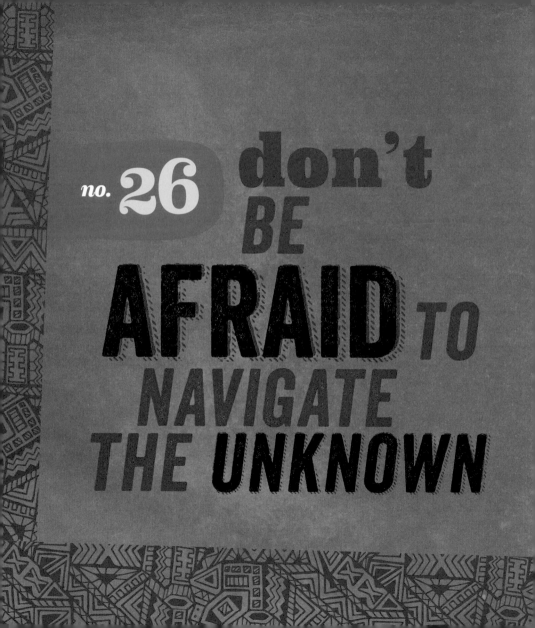

who among us

doesn't love to watch young people compete in the National Spelling Bee each year? The memories of my own participation as a child are fond ones—although I still have occasional nightmares about the word that cost me a championship many years ago. *Parapet*. I put two *r*'s in the word. Wrong.

In any event, it's an absolute joy to watch those young folks performing bravely in such a grueling competition. They've studied and prepared all they can. And yet when they step to the microphone for their turn, they have no idea which word is going to get thrown at them.

We spend significant amounts of time in our lives—maybe even more often than not—trying to navigate and negotiate the unknown. For too many of us, there's something about being unsure that causes us to be afraid, and we are paralyzed by it.

Yet all of us are going to come up against things that arrive out of left field. We won't know what the variables are; we have no control over when something might happen and no clue as to how it's going to affect us.

Having been blindsided myself time and again, I have simply had to learn that you can't be afraid to navigate and negotiate with the unknown. Whether we like it or not, it's coming. I dare say there's a chance it may cause pain, suffering, or destruction in our lives.

Yet I've come to the conclusion that the best—and sometimes only—thing we can do is to prepare

ourselves as well as possible, and accept this inevitability rather than fear it.

Besides accepting that the unknown is out there, it's essential to get yourself some insurance. For me, that comes from my faith. The essence of the human condition, at its very core, is a cry for help.

None of us can walk this journey alone.

For each of us, it means having a belief system about the world that gives us a second center of gravity when the unknown knocks us off the one we've built with our day-to-day lives.

Understand that you can't go it alone. That's why it's so critical to have meaningful, valuable relationships with family and friends. At their best, these are the people who provide strength to us. Reaching out to them will help you survive the ambiguities associated with crossing from uncertainty to assurance.

There also comes a recognition at some point—once the fear is gone—that as scary and intimidating as the unknown can be, it can be exhilarating and inspirational as well. In fact, I've ended up doing some of my best work up on that high wire.

That's what the youth who excel at the National Spelling Bee have realized at a young age, and that's what draws us to watch them in real time as they succeed, advance, win, and master the contest.

We will all meet the challenge of the unknown in unique ways. It's important to remember that if we're able to, we should enjoy the ride.

no. 27

YOU
CAN
DO
ANYTHING,

used to say to me all the time, "Tavis, baby, you can do anything, but you can't do everything."

Of course as a child I was so self-confident, I thought I *could* do everything. Even to this day, friends say that I do everything I put my mind to.

It's nice to get a little compliment like that, but it's not true. My grandmother was right. I've had to develop a sense of my inner strengths and weaknesses, my abilities and limitations.

I believe that individuals, just like corporations, need to perform a SWOT—strengths, weaknesses, opportunities, threats—assessment on themselves. I do mine on my birthday each year. I've concluded that, if you're paying attention, you'll notice that these change over time, in ways both subtle and dynamic.

What doesn't change is that the only chance any of us have in making it in this world, professionally or personally, is to play to our strengths.

In any contest, challenge, or test, who wins by playing to their weaknesses?

Ultimately, the only person who can know what those characteristics are is you. You've got to be vigilant about accepting or rejecting what people around you say you're good and bad at. You are ultimately the decider-in-chief. Weigh your instincts with the opinions of others in arriving at an accurate assessment. Eventually, the "aha" moments will tell you what your strengths and weaknesses truly are.

When he was recording in the studio, Frank Sinatra would never let anybody tell him that something was good if he knew it could be better. He was aware of what the strengths and weaknesses of his songs were, and how important it was to play to those strengths. If the sound he wanted wasn't quite there yet—no matter what anyone else thought—he'd make everybody record the song again. And again. As many times as it took until Sinatra was convinced it was great.

Getting to the point where your sense of your own capabilities is finely tuned takes time and practice. At public speaking engagements, I know when I've killed it and when I haven't—nobody has to tell me. I can also now tell when a standing ovation isn't genuine. Sometimes an audience gives what I call the "courtesy standing O." Another type of response is when an audience is reserved, yet you know the speech has had a deep impact—no standing ovation required.

A deeply intuitive sense of your strengths alerts you to the difference between these things. You know when you've done your best work and when you haven't. But the only way to get consistently better at anything is to listen to yourself and to objectively assess your actions, play to your strengths, and—when your weaknesses interfere with your game—learn how to not make the same mistakes again.

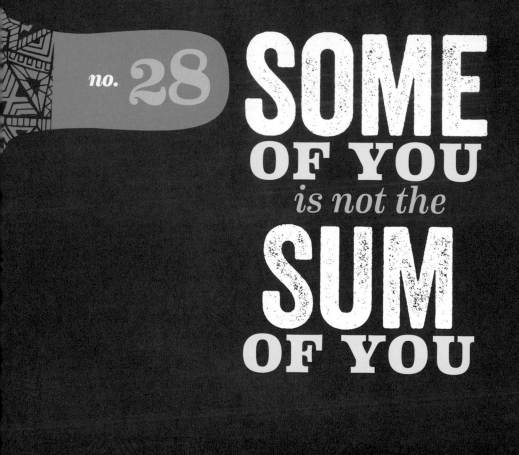

no. 28

SOME
OF YOU
is not the
SUM
OF YOU

i believe
there is no
difficulty in life

that we cannot recover from. I believe this because I believe in the promise of Christ's blood on the cross on Calvary—there is always redemption.

But it's not just a matter of faith. It's possible to live a life not judged exclusively on one decision, circumstance, or event. Even former president Richard Nixon, who was impeached and forced to resign from the highest office in the land after being involved in the Watergate scandal, later regained a measure of respect as an elder statesman.

I've come to understand that *some* of you is not the *sum* of you. We all have moments of good and bad, up and down, embarrassment, frustration, loss, maybe even tragedy. What matters is consistency.

Cal Ripken, Jr., is considered one of the greatest and most durable baseball players of all time. He was an MVP, an All-Star, and a World Series champion. But what Ripken is really known for is holding the Major League Baseball record for consecutive games played, at 2,632. He wasn't great every night in the ballpark—there were games where errors were made, balls were dropped, and he struck out every time at the plate. But we don't remember any of that. We remember his consistency.

To paraphrase the great Dr. Martin Luther King, Jr.: If it falls your lot to be a street sweeper, sweep the streets like Michelangelo painted pictures, like Shakespeare wrote poetry, like Beethoven composed music.

Now, that is a high calling!

Which is why, in a hit-it-and-quit-it world, consistency matters.

It is by keeping a day-in-and-day-out consistency and focus that we build a legacy. Make this your life's goal, and the rewards will be plentiful.

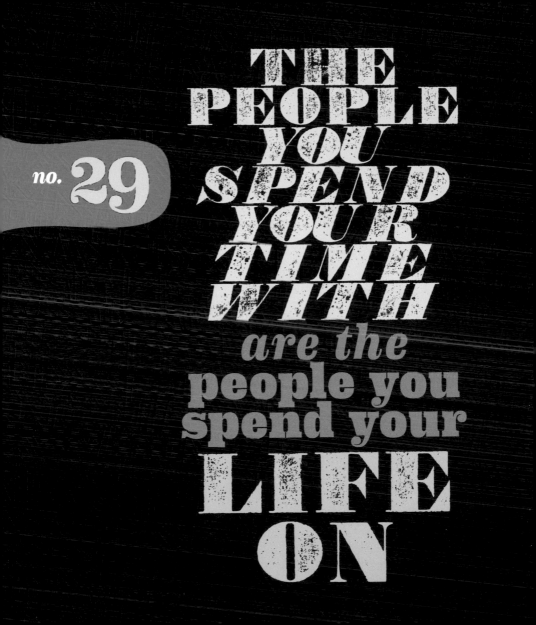

no. 29

THE PEOPLE YOU SPEND YOUR TIME WITH are the people you spend your LIFE ON

I consider myself a *good* judge of character.

I don't allow myself to deal with much nonsense, either. But there are certain friendships, certain relationships that I look back on and think, *I can't believe I spent four years in that situation.* On the other hand, I realize I should have worked harder at other relationships, that I would have personally benefited from spending more time with certain people.

The sad reality is that you can't change what you've already done. Life, as I've said, is more about memories than milestones. We create happy memories when we're around the people we are in harmony with, who bring us joy. Memories come courtesy of those you choose to spend your time with, where you choose to spend time with them, and the point in your life you were at when you did.

That's why it's so important to remember that the people you spend your time with are the people you spend your life on.

I have a friend whom I talk to regularly. This guy is amazing. He packs so much into every single weekend that it astounds me. It's just a litany of stuff. We were talking about it once and he said, "Tavis, you and I, we have the same number of hours in our weekend. I just use mine better." It occurred to me then that my friend's lifestyle worked well for him, but probably wouldn't for me.

We might not be destined to have the same number of years in our lives, but we do have the same number of hours in our days. How and with whom are you spending yours?

Remember that people will waste your time if you let them.

When you spend time with the wrong person, you can never retrieve those hours again.

My gauge has been this: If the person in question is not pouring good into my life in any significant or meaningful way, I should probably spend less time with him or her. I'm probably wasting my precious life on someone not worthy of it. As I've gotten older, I've learned not to spend any appreciable time with someone who's not helping me be a better man. Every day of my life, I'm committed to trying to do better. The people who don't support me in that goal are no longer allowed in my personal space.

Too often we get caught up in other people's foolishness, which leads us to become accomplices in their debauchery. You should choose to be around people who celebrate you, not who simply tolerate or use you. I can promise you that it's a much better way to spend your time—and your life.

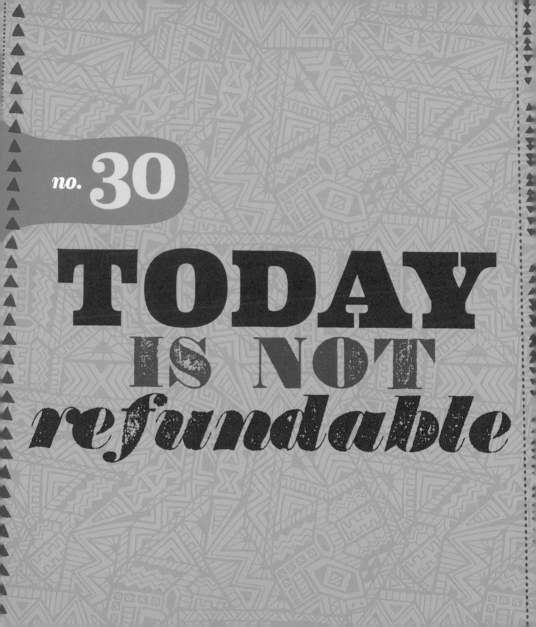

no. **30**

TODAY
IS NOT
refundable

Before we buy something,

we usually take the time to find out whether or not it's refundable. This fact plays a key part in our decision to acquire it or not. It changes our perspective on the value of a product and affects the amount of time we spend researching it. It involves a completely different psychology.

I patronize certain stores because I know that if I don't like an item I buy, I can return it for a full refund. Nordstrom is one of these stores. I don't spend too much time thinking about an item's price there, or whether it's exactly right, or whether I'll still wear it in six months or a year. If I realize that I don't, in fact, like a pair of shoes I bought, for instance, I bring them back anytime, no questions asked, and get my money back.

Now compare this to how we purchase cars, or our homes. We spend much more time gathering information on sedans or neighborhoods than we do on shoes not just because of the vast difference in price; it's because they cannot simply be returned once we sign for them on the dotted line. A car's value immediately begins to depreciate the moment you drive the vehicle off the lot—no wonder we do so much comparison shopping and test-driving and asking for advice on different models. A home is where we want to be completely comfortable, but its location affects the distances we travel to get to and from school and work, and is often a big part of our investment strategy

for our later years. Mortgages are not something to trifle with.

How much more attentive, thoughtful, and earnest should we be, then, about the decisions we make on a daily basis about the way we live our lives?

Because if a car doesn't come with a money-back guarantee, then this day—*today*—is undoubtedly not refundable. Today begins at midnight and ends 24 hours later. After that, it's gone forever.

How we decide to live each day of our lives should be one of the most important of all the decisions we make, but so many of us approach each new day with a cavalier ndifferent attitude. We lollygag, procrastinate, show up late here and here, forget this, put off that, go to bed late, and get up way behind schedule.

All that cavalier behavior would change if you knew that today was going to be your last—you'd put a different valuation on it.

The brilliant Reverend Gardner C. Taylor taught a prayer that helps me focus on filling each nonrefundable day with my best: "When the evening comes and the night falls, I want to look back on this day and see something that I've done that I can present to You, Lord, that might not make me feel so ashamed."

Each day is as precious as your last, because one of these days it *will* be. We can't take for granted, then, the fleeting, nonrefundable time that is given to us. Being mindful of the invaluable nature of each day will help make all of us better people.

sometimes
YOU HAVE TO
no. 31
▸▸▸▸▸▸▸▸▸▸▸▸▸▸
FIGHT
▸▸▸▸▸▸▸▸▸▸▸▸▸▸
WITH YOUR
FRIENDS

For *obvious reasons,*

when we think about fighting, we think about doing so with our enemies. But I've learned that sometimes you have to fight with your friends too.

I'm not talking about coming to blows or even fighting with the intent to hurt someone's feelings. I'm referring to being engaged in serious debate and principled argument. Sometimes friends fight over a deeply held belief, be it political, spiritual, or prejudicial. Sometimes it's over one's worldview, or over a personal ideology. Whatever it is, there come points in our lives when we need to fight with our friends.

Because sometimes your friends aren't right in action, word, or deed. When you believe they're wrong, you've got to be willing to fight with them. Engage them, press them, challenge them to reexamine their assumptions, and help them expand their inventory of ideas.

As I've said, I surround myself only with people who can help me become a better man. If your friends don't have any interest in improving themselves in meaningful ways or aren't willing to have difficult conversations sometimes, then are they really your friends?

Do you want to be around people who aren't willing to try to look at the world differently from time to time?

What I've had to learn the hard way is that good friends aren't obligated to do everything you want, when you want it, and how you want it done. If they choose to exercise their independence, it doesn't mean you need to cast them aside. It's one thing to have an uncomfortable conversation with a friend who's willing to engage with you and listen to your point of view, and quite another to acknowledge that you can't change his or her mind or make that person apply your beliefs to his or her own life. At that point, you can either let go of the argument altogether or decide to continue the fight another time. Every situation is different.

The consequence of not engaging in these intellectual and spiritual tussles with the people we choose to spend our time with and our life on is that the issues we avoid become a callus that builds over time. Before you know it, that thing is so hardened there's no way you can grind it down. It may mean that it's time to say good-bye to that friend—which could perhaps turn out to be a gift—but now I know that you can't be afraid of at least trying to have the conversation. The alternative—doing nothing and letting the frustration build—only leads to bigger problems.

It's critical to remember one thing, even during a heated debate or dialogue. It's something I believe with every fiber of my being, but that I have to consciously remind myself of every day.

I believe, if we try hard enough, there's nothing in life that we're called on to say or do that we cannot find a way to say or do in love.

Now, I'm the first to admit that isn't easy. When you argue with your friends over principles, your tone needs to reflect love. Otherwise, the message and the meaning become lost and the whole venture can be scuttled by pettiness and spite.

These are your friends, after all, and if the friendship is strong, it will survive occasional tests and become even stronger.

no. 32

some
SUFFERING
is
UNAVOIDABLE

Few of us ever think

our lives will be burdened by suffering. We focus on the good times—the fun, the laughter, the festivities. That's just how we process life.

We usually don't care to reflect much on the fact that some amount of suffering is unavoidable. But, in truth, it's just as much a part of life as the good times are.

Earlier in my career, I used to play a game with myself. Could I be consistently right? I set certain rules for myself: I didn't speak about topics I didn't know very well. I tried to avoid absolute statements. I certainly wouldn't tell an outright lie.

I honestly believed it would be possible for me to be right 99.9 percent of the time.

Turns out, I was completely wrong. Even if I played by those rules, there were times I made mistakes. There were times I slipped up, when erroneous statements came out of my mouth that I could not take back. Whether I liked it or not, I was going to make mistakes and I was going to bring suffering into my life because of it.

We are all emotional creatures. None of us is both human and divine; we are only human. In moments of rage, frustration, hubris, arrogance, or narcissism, we say and do things we wish we hadn't.

The good thing is that we can minimize the suffering we bring on ourselves because of these moments by exercising self-control and thoughtfulness.

But there will be things in your life that you do not see coming or that you have no control over. They'll blindside and sucker punch you, and that leads to unavoidable suffering. We've already talked about how to love is to suffer. That is often an unavoidable suffering— whether because it's your family that none of us gets to choose, or because your affections for someone else have taken complete control and aren't reciprocated.

Maybe it's a job that suddenly disappears through no fault of your own. It could be the unexpected loss of a close loved one. In love and life, in work and play, some suffering is unavoidable.

Like in baseball, sometimes you're going to get hit just because you're standing in the batter's box. Those fastballs come out of the pitcher's hand and occasionally—but usually not intentionally—you get plunked.

If you want to play in this game called life, you have to be able to deal with the pain of getting beaned—and then shake it off.

That can be easier said than done, believe me. Life will give you plenty of fastballs on its own, so look to minimize the self-inflicted suffering. When it happens, take responsibility, fix the problem, and move on.

Learn to recover as quickly as possible from both types of suffering. Build up your psychic and spiritual defenses against the unseen and the unavoidable, and cultivate thoughtfulness so you don't inflict unnecessary suffering on yourself. Sometimes pain takes time to heal, but don't let it stop you in your tracks. Unresolved suffering will shut you down if you let it.

no. 33 DON'T
FREAK OUT—
FIGURE
IT OUT!

So many *gifts* come along with age.

I can almost promise you, for instance, that at a certain point you'll start developing a sense of calm when it comes to managing crises.

This may seem oxymoronic, because when we think about crisis the last idea that comes to us is remaining calm. But after living through a lot of tough situations over the years, I gradually stopped freaking out when they happened. My best defense for overcoming panic is to figure out what to do about it. When you freak out, you lose all sense of perspective and logic; your ability to make good decisions almost completely disappears.

One way we can maintain calm is to understand the difference between a problem or an inconvenience and a true crisis.

A crisis is being told you have cancer and only 45 days to live. A crisis is a tornado or hurricane heading straight for your house. A crisis is a stock market crash that causes your life savings to disappear overnight.

Things that we tend to label "crises"—getting fired from a job, not getting a promotion, botching a sales presentation, losing a bidding war on a house, having your electricity turned off or your bank account frozen, seeing your kids act up at school or at home—they're not really full-fledged crises even though they seem like it at the time. Remaining calm is the most effective way to navigate any dangers or problems they present.

It took me years to figure this out. Today I know that a lot of what's behind my ability to stay calm in almost any situation is simply a wealth of experience. A part of me believes that staying calm during the storms of life is something that's happened as I've become more mature and levelheaded in general.

But I also know it's not just about experience or age. It's about how you approach a crisis situation. Let your intuition guide you as to how to work through problems and inconveniences in the best way possible.

Learning to stay calm about small things will also help you stay calm when you're faced with a major issue.

Save your energy for real crises.

Another thing I've learned is that sometimes, even before I can begin to freak out about something, it's already been worked out. My faith reinforces that viewpoint. But take it a step further: If you've already stockpiled faith in yourself, then you'll have the tenacity to get yourself out of a mess, or to recognize the path that's already been laid before you. But the surest way to miss the road signs and amplify the problems you're facing is to freak out.

Sometimes the cosmos does work in your favor—you just have to remain calm and look at the stars to see how they're aligned.

no. **34**

YOU'RE
ENTITLED TO
nothing

There are some things in life that we deserve,

. . . .

and others that we have to demand.
I believe that each of us deserves
respect. And if you don't get it, then
you have to demand it—we are all
owed this basic human right.

I believe that, in this country,
you deserve access to health care.
You deserve a high-quality education. You deserve to live in a neigh-
borhood free of crime. You deserve
to not live next to a toxic dump. You
deserve a job with a living wage, not
just a minimum wage. We should be
demanding these things if we aren't
getting them.

I fear, though, that social media,
reality television, and the instant
gratification we receive in so many

ways in the world today are making us a culture of narcissists. There's been a shift in expectations.

People expect things to just happen for them now— whenever they want it, however they want it—and they don't show any gratitude when they're granted their wish.

I've become increasingly concerned over the rising sense of entitlement in this country. I've encountered it all over the place: as interacting with people as an entrepreneur, and certainly through my time spent with celebrities and personalities of all kinds through my broadcast work.

This is one of the only lessons in this book I can say I've learned by engaging with and observing the lives of others, and not through my own personal experience. I grew up not even feeling entitled to an hour alone in the bathroom, let alone second or third helpings at the dinner table or expensive clothes.

What's tripping me up is that it's not just the well-to-do, the lucky, or the elite who feel entitled—it's everyone. I say all the time that you can't make demands unless you're *in* demand. And yet everyone, regardless of whether they're in demand or not, somehow feels entitled these days to make demands simply because they believe they're

So many "ordinary" people feel this way, those yet to make any meaningful contributions. They don't have fame or notoriety. They don't have name recognition. They don't have leverage. They don't have multiple degrees. They haven't invented anything important.

The problem is that you can't command your future into existence. There are no shortcuts. You have to work to make success happen, and even then it is not guaranteed, let alone instantaneous.

You cannot demand a job for which you are not qualified. You cannot demand a salary that your experience doesn't justify. You cannot demand power and control and authority that you aren't ready to wield. And you cannot demand to be let into the club of exclusivity simply because you think you've got a great profile on LinkedIn—it's not your club!

I don't know anyone who likes a person who acts entitled. That behavior isn't worthy of respect. On the other hand, people always respect folks who deliver. I'm around people who love those who work hard, who prove themselves, earn their power and respect, and earn their own way in the world. And who do it with integrity. That's the path to true success.

But you've got to put in the work—you're entitled to nothing.

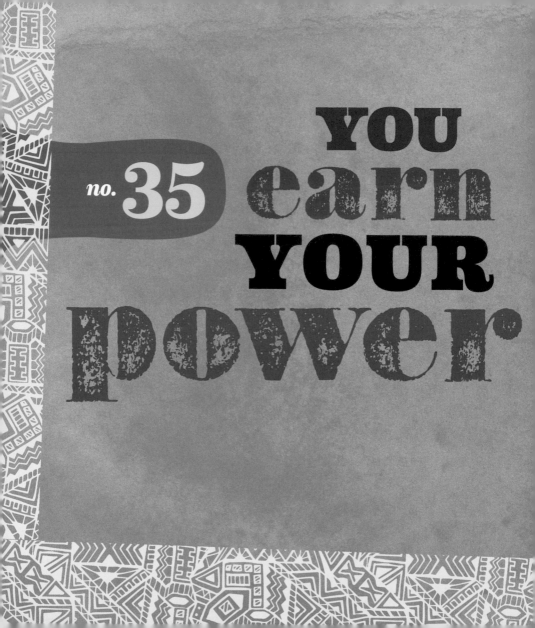

no. **35**

YOU earn YOUR power

These days, **too many people have taken Malcolm X's mantra,** "**By any means necessary,**" *and turned it on its head.*

They're determined to get to the top—and they're willing to get that power any way they can.

Undercutting, sidestepping, overstepping, taking people out at the knees, or just going over someone's head—whatever it takes.

Too many people today believe that's how real power is attained. And if they are able to make that tactic work in their favor, when they get the power they're after, they realize they don't have what it takes to make it effective: respect. When you take moral shortcuts on your way to the top in a quest for power, it never lands you where you really want to be.

Like the Bible says, "What does it profit a man to gain the whole world and lose his soul?"

If you have power but no love, compassion, empathy, or interest in serving others, then you have an empty sort of power. A powerless power.

The lesson here is that you have to earn your power. When your actions warrant your being in power, that power comes along with a moral authority that you otherwise don't have. To get anything of meaning, purpose, or value accomplished, you need to have some real power. But power is truly effective only if it is built on decency.

I've seen so many people chasing success and power when what they really want is significance. Their efforts are misguided. People flaunt and flex, posture and position, all in a quest for power—but for what? What do they plan to use it for, or do with it?

The power most people crave is an external power— to influence, impact, and control others.

Most people aren't nearly as interested in inner power. Self-control and self-reflection are holy inner strengths. I've realized that if more people were in possession of these, there'd be a lot less craving for external power in the world.

History is replete with examples of people who held high positions but were shown to be empty, deficient, morally bankrupt, and self-loathing. They tried to compensate for those internal deficiencies by gaining as much external power as they could. I often wonder how different Adolf Hitler's life—and the lives of the six million people he murdered—might have turned out had he been accepted into that art school in Vienna. We can never know, because any internal fortitude he might have used to pursue that dream of being an artist succumbed to the corrosive effects of a deviant and cruel personality.

The road to earning external power begins with mastering inner power. Taking this path prevents self-manipulation, self-exploitation, and self-aggrandizement—the early warning signs of a hunger for power accrued for the wrong reasons and in the wrong way.

By putting in time and overtime, seeking truth, making good decisions, being earnest in your dealings, and not cheating or embezzling, lying or stealing, you'll set yourself on the path to acquiring the type of power and authority that allow you to make a humane and bold difference in the world.

no. **36**

FORTUNE
and
FAME
don't
fix
flaws

You hear it all the time: Money doesn't make you happy.

I live and work in Los Angeles and interview famous and wealthy people all the time. I now know this saying is more than just a platitude.

Look, every one of us wants to have and achieve a certain modicum of success. Let me be the first to tell you that there's nothing wrong with being successful. I have worked really hard at it myself! But I worry that too many people are chasing success and not greatness.

There are so many people in the world who've become wildly successful, though they will never be regarded as being great. But, conversely, you can never be great without being successful.

Let me explain.

I believe that the definition of success is different for each of us. Oftentimes, the highest reward is not what we receive for our efforts, but who we become by them.

Success is about what you have; greatness is about who you are.

As part of my philanthropic work through the Tavis Smiley Foundation, I expose thousands of youth all across America to a leadership development curriculum. For years I would go around the room in training sessions, asking the participants, one by one, what they wanted to be when they grew up. Eventually, I realized that was the wrong question. It's not about *what* you want to be, but *who* you want to be. The former question is external, the latter is internal; the first is superficial, the second is more substantive.

Who are you, really?

It seems to me that's the ultimate question life is trying to get us to wrestle with.

Loving and serving humanity— that's how Dr. Martin Luther King, Jr., defined greatness. "Everybody can be great because everybody can serve . . . You only need a heart full of grace. A soul generated by love," he said.

Disturbingly, the threshold for so-called success keeps getting lower in our culture. More and more, people are becoming famous for being famous—they haven't accomplished anything; they haven't mastered anything or created anything meaningful or worthy.

Now everyone in the age of reality television wants—and feels they deserve—fortune and fame for doing nothing. They see a bunch of other folks on television every day who themselves are famous for doing basically nothing.

Let me share a secret: This kind of vapid and hollow "success" might bring fortune and fame, but it doesn't fix your internal flaws, whether they be emotional, spiritual, psychological, or familial.

If you were defective before you got famous, you'll still be that way when you get everything you *think* you want.

And once this happens, the flaws only get worse. Fame and fortune amplify them. So be careful what you ask for.

Be a person of character first. Remember: Your character won't lead you anywhere it can't keep you, sustain you, or protect you.

Character matters.

fall
FIGHTING

In life, we don't just fight for today.

We don't fight for a week or a month. We don't even fight for just a year. As a matter of fact, in life we fight, we struggle, all the way through to the end.

I believe it can be a beautiful struggle—but it's a struggle nonetheless.

The underappreciated civil rights heroine Fannie Lou Hamer once said, "If I fall, I'll fall five feet, four inches forward in the fight for freedom."

The truth is that during our lifetime we are intermittently going to fall. We're going to fail, we're going to trip up, and we're going to get knocked off our squares. That's part of the struggle.

It's important to remember that there is no utopian moment when the fight, the struggle, ends. You're going to be fighting the good fight all the way through. Don't put off goals and aspirations simply because you're struggling—there is, as it's said, no time like the present.

The truth is, even in the good times there's still going to be struggle.

To a person, everybody I know who has achieved a high level of success says the same thing when I ask, "Is it harder to get it, or harder to keep it?"

It's always harder to keep it.

Reaching your goal—whether you're the biggest pop star in the world or finally getting that promotion at work you've been angling for year after year—doesn't mean the battle is over. In many ways, it's just beginning. It's time to defend the gains you made, even as you look to the next level. And a lot of times you'll have people nipping at your heels each time you reach a higher status. Look at it this way: If you don't have the ball, nobody will try to tackle you. Success of any kind invites competition, which is why you've got to keep focused on what's next. Consolidate your gains and move forward.

It's crucial to be aware that failures will come. How you respond to them is almost always more important than the failure itself.

Over the course of many decades, I've learned that when you fall it's best to pay attention to Fannie Lou Hamer's wisdom: fall forward. Even as we take those inevitable spills, we should be looking to cover some extra territory. In the best of circumstances it'll be a righteous fall, when we fight for something greater than ourselves.

CONFORMITY CURBS *freedom of* THOUGHT

I AM NOT
a conformist.

Nor was any great historical figure or icon that I respect.

We live in a society of cultural, artistic, political, and technological plagiarists. There are too many impersonators and not enough innovators in the world—too many copies and not enough originals.

In spite of this, our basic biology defies this drive for conformity.

The Human Genome Project taught us that we're all basically the same. The billions of people on this planet share the same essential genetic code and makeup. Yet it's easy to see that we're all also unique—just look at your thumbprint. Not a single person in the world has quite the same one as you.

And as sure as your thumbprint is uniquely yours, your voice in this world, too, is unlike anyone else's.

It's vital that you make that voice heard. That can't happen if you become a conformist.

Allowing your voice to be drowned out by the thoughts and ideas of others means that the best part of you never surfaces. That's one of the reasons why education is important. The purpose of education isn't to simply help you pick the right answer on a test; it's to help you learn to be a critical thinker. I've never had reason to dissect a rat since I graduated high school, and I haven't had to solve an algebra equation since then, either. But the point of learning those things wasn't to prepare me to do them. The point was to get me to think critically.

Learning means thinking for yourself, so that for the rest of your life you'll be free to come to your own conclusions and express yourself with confidence.

When you succumb to conventional wisdom or the opinion of the status quo, you sacrifice the ability to contribute your own ideas and to have an impact on others. Conformists lose the chance to share the best of themselves with the world. Critical thinking allows you to discover whether conventional wisdom will work for you.

And that's okay. When you think for yourself, when you develop your own belief system, when you create a mission statement for your life, you develop your own voice. You're creating an original personality capable of making fresh, meaningful contributions in this world.

Early on in his career, Ray Charles struggled with his musical identity. He was trying to sound like Nat King Cole. But the world already had Cole's creative genius. What it was waiting for was the original voice and style of Ray Charles. Once he created his own signature sound—by feeling the words from the depths of his own heart—he found his audience. Everything changed for him then.

Creativity and conformity cannot coexist.

no. 39

LIVE
BY YOUR
HOPES,

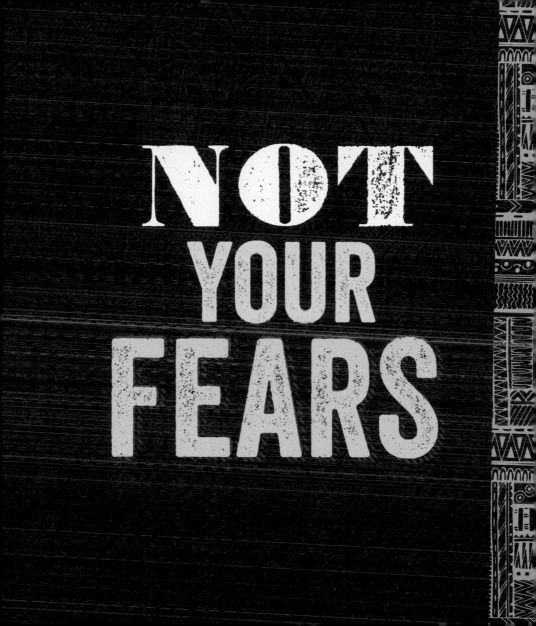

These days,

there seem to be a lot more things that make us fearful than make us hopeful. This is particularly true for people living in crime-ridden or polluted communities. Or where work is hard to come by, schools and homes are crumbling, and gentrification is collapsing the spirits of neighborhoods. When quality food is nowhere to be found and affordable public transportation fails to operate, it's easy for fear to dominate people's lives.

There are so many whose lives are entrenched in communities that are constricted and contained by fear. This situation is pandemic.

Your environment plays a big role in how you feel on a day-to-day basis, but you're also responsible for determining your own mind-set.

How can you make good choices about anything if you're afraid of the results or the possible consequences you're going to face?

Life has taught me that I've never made a good decision based on fear. On the other hand, hope has always guided my wisest decisions. I regret once staying in a business deal too long for fear of hurting my friend and partner. I lost the business and the friendship. Conversely, I have no regrets about any career move I've ever made based on the hope of my future.

When anxiety drives us, decisions are reached far too quickly and inside a vacuum. We lose sight of the whole picture facing us, focus on the wrong things, and fail to give enough thought to the decision itself. We come to a conclusion without ever looking for an alternate exit strategy.

Think about how many people stay in relationships that stopped working long ago. Their reasons range from being afraid of losing the security of having a partner to simply not wanting to be alone—and everything in between. In any case, fear motivates their decision to stay. It's hard for them to hope they'd be happier if they walked away.

I have a friend who recently took a buyout from a big job in Chicago.

She'd worked at her company for 24 years and hated almost every minute of it! Yet she admitted that if she hadn't been offered the buyout, she'd still be there, unhappy and crippled by the fear of what might happen if she left. It didn't occur to her to change that fear to hope, which would have liberated her to look for a job that was meaningful to her and made her happy.

How many people do we know who've been living in the same place for years, even though the environment has been dragging them down? The fear of change, of starting fresh, and especially the fear of failure so often keeps people locked in to the same patterns, day in and out.

Show me a success story and I'll show you a situation invariably driven by hope, not by fear. It's amazing what the power of hope can do, but it requires unlocking yourself from the cage of fear you're trapped in. You have to consciously let the power of hope manifest itself in your life.

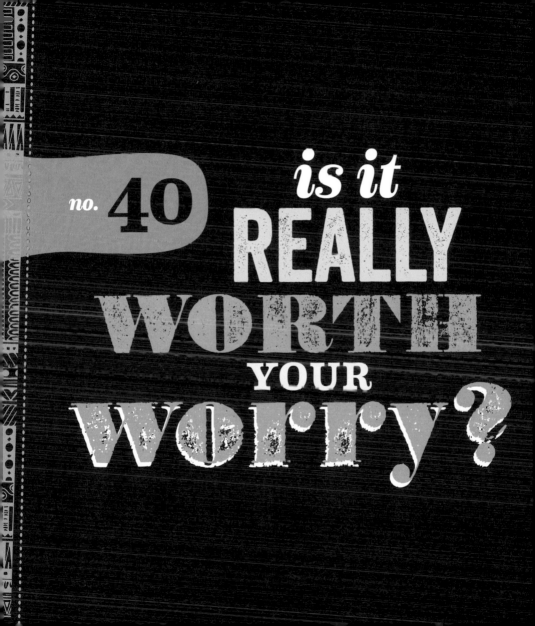

no. 40 *is it* REALLY WORTH YOUR worry?

REMEMBER

that Bobby McFerrin song from the late '80s "Don't Worry, Be Happy"? The song is a really good philosophy for life in just four words, and it won Grammy awards for Song of the Year and Record of the Year, because it struck a note of hope and optimism with people. Not unlike the more-recent hit song "Happy" from the artist Pharrell Williams.

I am not one of those people who believe you shouldn't worry about anything. I also don't believe that our only choice is between worrying about everything and worrying about nothing. Worrying about nothing makes you cavalier, and worrying about everything makes you neurotic.

We all know people who we'll call "worrywarts"—folks consumed with apprehension about everything. The problem is, we each have only so much bandwidth in our lives. And worrying is like the streaming video of our emotional and spiritual Internet connection—it crowds out our ability to work on what we need to get done.

That's because worry and work occupy the same space in your head and your heart.

You can't do both at the same time. Worrying limits your creativity; it shuts down your capacity for innovation and inspiration. Think of it as a pie chart: If worrying takes up 80 percent of your time, the entire balance of your existence has to fight for the remaining 20 percent.

You have to decide what is actually worth your worry. Each of us has to develop a process by which we determine what's important enough to become stressed over and what is not, in the end, truly worrisome.

Nowadays I don't worry about things I cannot control. Concern should be commensurate with your level of control. If you did all you could to prepare for that test or that job interview or that presentation at work, then once you've put all the effort you can into a situation, let it go. Free your head and your heart from worry and move on. You'll know the outcome soon enough.

If you aced the test or got the job or nailed the presentation, then allow yourself to revel in your success as you prepare for the next challenge. And if you didn't do as well as you hoped but you've freed yourself from worry, you've already buffered yourself against being crushed; you're already moving on to the next thing.

Let's be clear: I do worry over the things I *can* control. But even then, once I become aware that I'm feeling anxious, I've learned how to turn it around. I ask myself, *How can I approach this situation creatively? How can I be innovative with this? If I made a mistake, how can I recover from it and move on?*

This way, the worry transforms itself into action. And the only way the situation you're worried about is going to change is if you work your way through it step-by-step. Solutions present themselves to us much faster when worry isn't part of the equation.

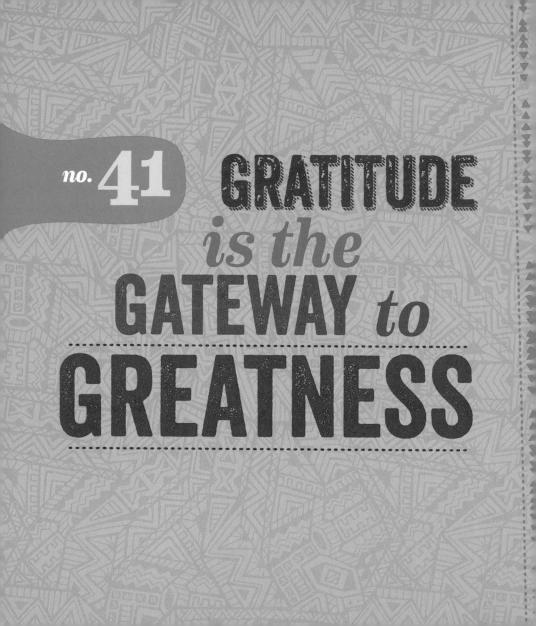

no. **41** GRATITUDE *is the* GATEWAY *to* GREATNESS

Too many people today lack gratitude.

From not saying "thank you" to the kind soul opening a door for us to showing deep social apathy toward the opportunities presented to us, it's evident we are living through a drought of gratitude.

Earlier I said that Quincy Jones had come up with a good definition of greatness: someone who is humble about creativity and gracious about success. But the path to greatness—the road that leads to a humble heart and a graceful spirit —passes through the gateway of gratitude.

That's not what most people think about when they ponder what it is that leads to greatness. They think it's who you know and how much money you have. They equate it with the kind of job you have or the car you drive. Throw in how many college degrees you've earned and what your zip code is, and you've arrived at our society's misguided, out-of-sync perception of what constitutes greatness.

We're given messages—or we're told by the media—that these superficial things can lead us to greatness.

Dr. King said nothing about cars, or jobs, or the square footage of your house, or the size of your paycheck. Greatness, to him, was about your capacity to love and serve people.

And he believed the gifts that we are born with give us everything we need. It is here that gratitude becomes key.

Every one of us comes into this world with a resident gift—some of us are blessed with a multitude of them. I'm a person of faith, so I believe these are gifts bestowed by God. But whatever your personal belief system is, we can all acknowledge that the possibilities waiting to be unleashed within all of us are instilled by some higher power.

An alarming number of people just don't understand that a capacity for goodness and greatness is a gift. You didn't gift it to yourself, either. You didn't birth yourself or nurture yourself, and you're not going to bury yourself when you die—we all rely on each other, from start to finish.

Everything starts with us being *given* something, from our very lives to our innate talents and abilities.

How dare we not have a sense of deep, abiding gratitude for these?

And when you come in contact with someone else's gift—expressed to you, given to you, shared with you—you would do well to show gratitude for that too. Whether a gift comes in the form of a brilliant performance at a concert or someone letting you into traffic on a busy street, show a little gratitude.

People give us gifts every day, but we barely recognize these gestures as bestowals of kindness, consideration, inclusion, creativity, or caring. Let's face it: Nobody *has* to speak to you, or include you, or acknowledge you, or love you. But they do—and isn't love the greatest gift of all?

Even the smallest amount of gratitude goes such a long way, and for a seemingly small investment, it has a huge payoff.

It can be as simple as using a "thank you" to close all your e-mails, or telling folks face-to-face that you appreciate them, as I do. A friend of mine calls everyone *Brother* and *Sister*. Another friend greets everyone with a hug. Those are the kinds of simple daily habits that set in motion the journey toward greatness.

If gratitude is the gateway to greatness, you'll still need to figure out the password for when you get there. What's going to be your ticket in?

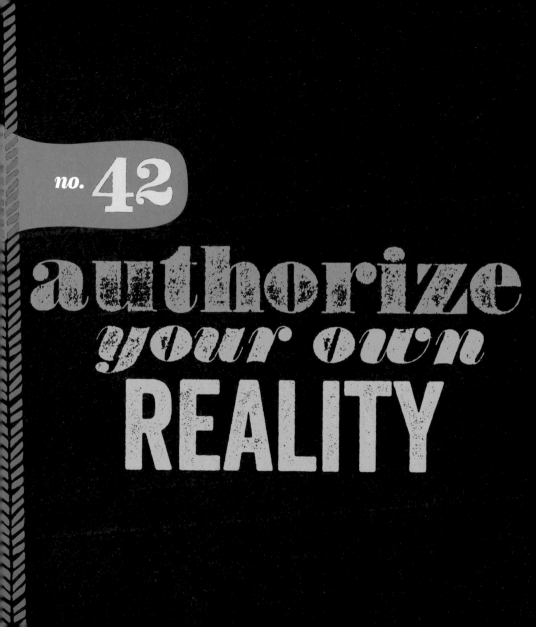

no. **42**

authorize
your own
REALITY

BOOKS ARE WRITTEN ABOUT PEOPLE
all the time.

There are authorized versions and unauthorized versions. (By the way, the book you're reading is most definitely the *authorized version!*)

Were someone to write the story of you, would they be telling the authorized version? Or would they be telling the version that's been decided upon and mandated by other people?

If you're living an unauthorized life, it's time to get to a place where you can authorize yours.

I've found that so many young people end up in a given career because their parents pushed them in a certain direction. Or they landed somewhere unsatisfying because a foolish guidance counselor steered them away from what they really wanted to do, claiming they weren't "qualified." This happens way too often in inner-city schools where administrators regularly diminish students' abilities.

We all know people who were raised in homes where they were never encouraged, where they were browbeaten and abused physically, mentally, or emotionally. Maybe you are one of those people whose parents told you that you would never go anywhere or amount to anything or accomplish anything.

You have to authorize your own reality.

To the people who've been subjected to racism or sexism or homophobia: It's time to authorize your own reality.

Don't star in a life written, produced, and directed by somebody else. You've got to become an independent production, unburdened by the decisions and demands and difficulties forced on you by other people.

It's your life. You tell the story.

There will inevitably be people in your life who will try to advance an unauthorized version of who you are. Once you've taken control of the script of your life story, you'll find yourself changing and growing and maturing. But there will still be people who'll want to keep you in some version of who you used to be, or who they thought you were, or who you were when you weren't your best self.

As a public figure, I've struggled with this. People come out of the woodwork to say, "I knew him when, and he was like this and that."

When the reality of who you once were or the life that you once lived is less admirable than it is today, all you can do is keep your chin up and keep marching.

Once you've reauthorized your reality, you've truly settled into your authentic, more substantial self.

Every person you come into contact with gives you a chance to treat them well, to engage with them, to respect, serve, and love them in a way that you might not have been able to 10 or 20 or even 30 years ago. Take the opportunity to help someone else begin writing the first chapter of his or her updated, self-authorized version of who he or she is today. This is a blessing that works both ways.

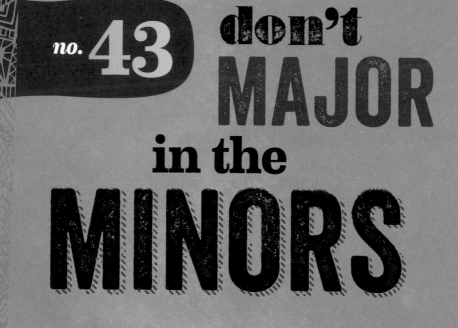

no. 43 don't MAJOR in the MINORS

Merriam-Webster's *dictionary defines* major *and* minor *in these ways:*

MAJOR means very important or large in number, amount, or extent.

MINOR means not very important or valuable; small in number, quantity, or extent; or not very serious.

Too many people major in the minors. They place importance on unimportant things. They treat small things as though they're significant. They elevate the frivolous to the serious.

These folks get stuck on small things and then find it hard to move beyond them—small projects, small insults, and small-minded people. For each of us, the definition of what constitutes the "minors" in our life is different. I've learned that we all have shifting perspectives on what percentage of our time and thought should be given to each minor circumstance.

You can identify the major things in your life by whether they pass some basic tests. In the greater scheme of things, is this situation going to make a difference a year from now? In five years, will you remember it at all? What impact does it *really* have on your life and the lives of the people you love?

I can think of so many things in my life that I thought were major when they happened. Now I can't believe I was so hung up on them at the time. Other folks don't even remember them. These incidents don't matter anymore, and they haven't changed my life or affected my livelihood.

When I was young, my granddad gave me some simple advice: Focus on the big things in life. Too often,

people fill their heads and hearts with a million little activities and commitments. It makes them feel like they've got a lot going on, but in the end they're left holding sand when they thought they were carrying a boulder.

Aim for big things: big goals, big dreams, and big aspirations. Seek out big, meaningful conversations and ideas. Get involved with inspiring, excited, engaged people, and socialize with them.

Connect yourself to something that's bigger than you.

These are the major components of a fulfilling life.

When you do this, your mind-set will shift. You'll find you don't focus on the small stuff—the petty insults and grudges, the chitter-chatter of small talk, the little mistakes or failings that act like booby traps for you. Your priorities will become clearer. Your vision for yourself and your life will come into sharper focus.

I've found this is something best learned young, when we feel like everything is going to matter forever. The first break-up, the first failed exam, the first job interview you flub— it all feels like the world's crashing in. But there'll be another relationship, another test to take, and a good job right around the corner. Don't hold a grudge, don't dwell on what's already passed, don't major in the minors—the big stuff is still ahead.

Life is not like a piano. A piano needs its minor keys—its sharps and flats—to be in tune, as well as its major keys. Playing a concerto? Then worry about the entire keyboard facing you. Working on life? Forget the minor keys and keep your fingers dancing.

no. **44**

SOMETIMES
WE ARE CALLED
TO DO
THINGS
WE CANNOT
do alone

SCORES OF PEOPLE WORK
with me every day to help make me the best brand possible.

None of us walks alone in this world. We are who we are because somebody loved us. Life is, by definition, a collaborative affair.

And sometimes in life we are assigned tasks—we are given responsibilities and duties, sometimes by our fellow human beings, sometimes by powers on high—that we cannot do on our own.

Think about someone like Beyoncé—she's a phenomenal talent and consummate stage performer. Every night that the curtain rises on her show, it is the accumulation of years of work, hundreds if not thousands of people's efforts, and the ability of a team to work together flawlessly. While you're singing along to all her greatest hits, a small army of talented, dedicated people is helping Beyoncé look and sound like the international pop star she is.

And Beyoncé wouldn't—*couldn't*—be who she is without them.

No matter how much talent or skill or passion you have, there will come a moment when, to be able to get to that place where you can do your finest work, you must rely on the gifts, the skills, and the commitment of others. And that's a beautiful thing! Success is achieved in this way.

Recognizing this truth is the only way to avoid becoming self-delusional. You can end up putting at risk all that you want to accomplish simply by having a demeanor or spirit that doesn't appreciate, value, and humble itself before the collaborative power that success is built on.

Too many folks think that the world actually does revolve around them, that they're the center of the spectacle and nothing or no one else matters. That they achieved their success on their own.

As my brother Dr. Cornel West likes to say, we are a culture of peacocks. We're all struttin' around, trying to get the world to look at us. But, in truth, peacocks strut because they can't fly.

If you really want to fly—if you really want to soar—you're going to need someone to help you. Whether it's for one person or for a team of 50, being grateful for collaboration adds to our humanity and is a profound component of success.

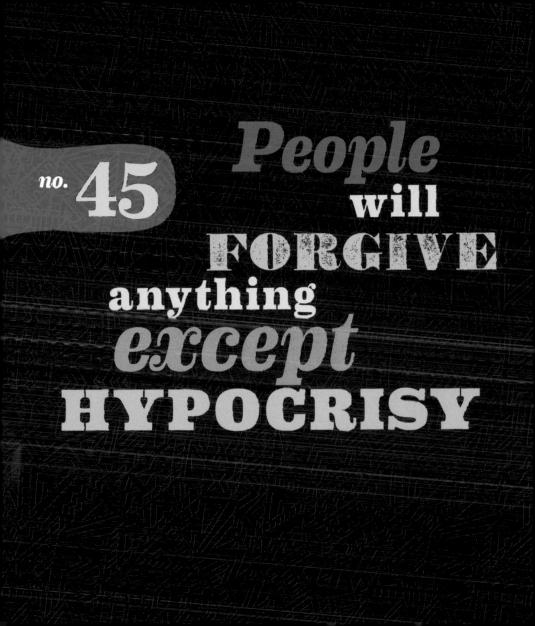

One of the
greatest joys
in my life

◀◀◀▶▶▶ ◀◀◀◀▶ ▶ ● ◀◀◀▶▶▶ ◀◀◀▶ ▶ ▶ ● ◀◀◀▶▶▶ ◀◀◀▶ ▶

has been my friendship with the incomparable Muhammad Ali. I consider him to be the greatest athlete who ever lived, not just because of his accomplishments in the boxing ring—which are arguably second to none—but also because of the courage he's shown outside the ropes. Believing the war in Vietnam to be morally reprehensible, Ali refused to join the military and fight. And because of his convictions he was stripped of his championship belt and lost much of his popularity with the American people.

During one of our many broadcast conversations I asked him, "Champ, you're the greatest boxer of all time and your name is revered the world over. To what do you attribute the fact that you are so beloved?"

He said, "It's because of just one thing. Whatever they think of me—love me or hate me—I have never lied to the American people."

No matter what the subject—race, politics, the war in Vietnam, religion—what Ali gave to the public was always straight, no chaser. I realized he was telling me that we can bounce back from almost everything—except hypocrisy.

We're all going to make mistakes. It's unavoidable. We forgive this, because it happens to all of us. But we have a problem with people who turn out not to be who we thought they were. There's a long list of public figures to choose from here—pick one!

We have a need to believe in people.

We crave strong, credible, inspired leaders. They help us deal with how complicated the world is.

Too often our leaders—who are just human beings that other human beings have elected, appointed, or anointed—see our impulse to hold them accountable for their actions or to critique perceived hypocrisy as an annoyance. In truth, it's an honor. And when those we've given this honor to turn out not to be who we thought they were, or who they said they were going to be, it deeply disappoints us. No one wants to be bamboozled, hoodwinked, or led astray. It shatters us.

We live in a world where many things and many people are fixated on the superficial. I've maintained for some years that this is why reality television took off the way it did. People could judge you in real time. Could you actually sing or dance? If you couldn't prove you had the skills to survive on an island, off you went.

Hypocrisy will get you voted off the island of life every time. That's hard to recover from. Avoid being hypocritical at all costs. When you increase your level of self-awareness, a tendency toward hypocrisy can be prevented before it becomes reality.

no. **46**

DON'T QUIT
DOUBLE
DOWN

I am not a quitter.
My second-grade teacher, Mrs. Vera Graft, saved me from that tendency.

I was the only Black kid in my class. One day Mrs. Graft called me over. I'd been throwing my hands up in frustration at things, refusing to finish my tasks.

"You are as capable, you are as smart, you are as gifted as anyone in this class, and you are not applying yourself," she told me. "I expect you to do the same high-quality work that others are doing because I know you're capable of it. You, my young friend, are going to have to quit quitting."

That was an important lesson for me. Now that I'm older, I understand that when things get difficult and challenging, when you're in crisis mode and nothing seems to be going right, only a strong constitution will keep you from quitting.

But what really makes the difference is not just that you don't quit. It's that you double down.

By this I mean you reach a point where you don't just rebound from a failure, you use it to leap forward. When you don't just recover, you go beyond. It's not about clawing yourself back to where you were before; it's about charging into a whole new space.

The moments in my life when things seemed the bleakest have also been when I found my greatest successes. As I look back at my life so far, I see that the darkest moments were immediately followed by spectacular illuminations.

What I've come to understand is that, in those moments, I doubled down. I aggressively applied myself to whatever project was in front of me, and I went over the top. There was something about coming close to quitting, to giving up, that motivated me to do more than I otherwise would.

To survive the bleak side of life, the dark times in our existence, you've got to double down.

The other side will be so glorious, you'll be so grateful you had the constitution to plow your way through.

Don't be content simply to survive. Most people are happy just to get on base after life throws a curveball at them. Don't let a single or even a triple be good enough in your life. Keep on swinging for the fences.

no. 47 don't let your RESERVATIONS become REGRETS

If I have the choice to *interview*

an 85-year-old or a 25-year-old, I'm
going to pick the elder every time.

I have nothing against young people. It's just that the older generation
has experienced so much more in
their lifetime. They have more real
knowledge to share and more wisdom to offer. There is an innate value
that comes with growing older.

I discover so much in conversations with my elders. I'm always fas-
cinated to discover how few regrets
one person may have, and how many
someone else may be harboring. And
why. To me there is nothing sadder
in the realm of human relations

than to sit and talk with an elderly person who has a series of regrets about which, due to age or physical condition or some other limitation, they can now do nothing.

Thanks to them, I've learned the value of living a life where reservations don't become regrets.

As I've said before, no matter how long we live, we're not going to get it all done. But there's a difference between making the most of what time we have—and of course the exact number of years allotted to us is a great mystery—and allowing our reservations, our misgivings, to turn into regrets.

In speaking with older folks, I've heard the same types of regrets repeated again and again. We can all learn from them.

I hear seniors frequently say, "If I'd known I was going to live this long, I would have taken better care of myself." They didn't exercise regularly, follow nutritious diets, or prioritize their health in general.

Relationships factor in to a lot of big regrets. I'm talking about love lost, apologies never offered, fights and disagreements that never got resolved, decades spent not speaking to someone over a petty incident. Generally, these relate to an inability to forgive or to repair a breach in a formerly steadfast friendship.

By contrast, when I talk to someone who lost a beloved partner after having spent several decades together, I don't hear about any regrets. They might miss the person terribly, but they don't lament anything about the time they spent together.

If you're giving love and you're receiving love, and it's all based in love, there can be no regrets.

Only the absence of love creates regrets.

Because I spend so much of my life traveling, for a long time the last thing I wanted to do with my free time was get on a plane. But one day I realized that my passion for seeing the world was going to be realized only by doing just that. As long as I honor my commitment to taking vacations abroad, I'll be able to keep those reservations from becoming regrets.

Making world travel a priority has both enlivened and enlightened me. I may be exhausted when I arrive, but there's nothing like the joy of discovering and experiencing a new place. Some of the greatest moments of my life have happened to me while traveling abroad. Talking with schoolchildren in China, visiting Mandela's prison cell on Robben Island in South Africa, being edified at the Sorbonne in Paris, France.

The lesson, then, is that when the love is flowing—between people in relationships, accompanying the indulgence in a passion like traveling, or for yourself when you take good care of your health—you will be living a life free of reservations and you'll have no regrets at the end.

bear
the
burden
of LOVE

The Bible doesn't command us to merely *like* our enemies. We are told to love them as we love ourselves.

I will freely admit that, of all the lessons in this book, the toughest one for me to learn—and re-learn— is how to bear the burden of loving people who don't love me back.

I've been able to get to this point in part thanks to the great poet Sonia Sanchez. She challenged a group of us one day to go 48 hours without expressing any kind of negativity toward another human being. For me, this not only meant stifling any pessimistic thoughts, but also not repeating something

I'd heard or forwarding a negative e-mail I'd received.

As simple of a task as it sounds, it wasn't. The thing I found most diffi-cult was not letting myself get pulled into other people's negativity. Even as I tried to avoid expressing my own, I had to struggle with the temp-tation to communicate or engage with disagreeable people around me.

The exercise was an eye-opener for me. I'm a public personality. I know what it means to be talked about and gossiped about, to be the victim of cyberbullying. This chal-lenge helped me to empathize with other people. Now I work assidu-ously not to gossip or to pass along gossip. I will sometimes cut people off in the middle of a conversation: *I don't want to hear it; I'm not trying to spread it.*

The more empathy we have—the more we stand in others' shoes—the easier it becomes to love people who don't love us back.

Too often we think that the only way to love is if it will be reciprocated.

The truth is that, in terms of our personal growth and development, that's not really the case.

We are in awe of the examples set by Dr. King, Ghandi, Nelson Man-dela. Yet we are puzzled by them. Each was slandered, maligned, abused physically and otherwise, denigrated, and manipulated by their enemies. And yet each one managed to love those who were so spiteful toward them. We recognize it, but we struggle to understand how they could bear the burden of loving those who did not love them back.

We struggle because emulating their example is so very difficult. We admire them because their reactions defy what we see in everyday behavior. Their ability to love represents the pinnacle of what we have achieved as a species. The truth is that we are at our absolute best if and when we find a way to be loving toward people who seemingly don't warrant it.

It is how we truly come into the fullness of our own humanity.

As I said, this has been life's most difficult lesson for me. I think most of us have to learn it over and over again. But taking even one step down the path toward learning to love those who might treat you spitefully is a step toward a more complete, compassionate, better you.

WORDS

need not be

WEAPONS

▶ ◀◀◀▶▶ ◀◀◀▶▶ ◀◀◀▶▶ ◀◀◀▶▶ ◀◀

More people have been injured by the **tongue** than by any other weapon in human history.

In our society, people tend to use words as weapons more often than they use them to heal or unite. The Internet and the rise of social media have given more power than ever to detrimental words, while providing cover and sanctuary for the worst abusers through easy anonymity.

I'm a broadcaster. I make my living using words. I know that words matter. We all have a slip of the tongue or a moment of verbal indiscretion, but there's a difference between off-the-cuff remarks and off-the-wall remarks.

Today, so much of what we put out into the world lives on forever and can be seen and heard by the masses. I learned this lesson the hard way. As detailed in my book *Fail Up*, I was once recorded saying things I didn't want other people to hear—but they did. Now I ask myself each day whether I would say what I'm thinking of saying if I knew there were hidden cameras or concealed microphones around. One moment of reflection can save you a lifetime of pain.

Maybe more important, I've learned of the degrading effect that inappropriate words can have on all of us.

There's no sophistication in them. I used to cuss, years ago, and one day I was just laying into someone—really unloading on this guy. He turned to me in the middle of my profane tirade and said, "With all that education, is that the best you can do? You're making me question the value of an Indiana University degree."

That stopped me cold. Dude checked me completely, without once having to resort to the kind of base vulgarity many of us practice every day.

What's truly sad is that so much good can come from language when it's used properly, when it's used for instruction instead of destruction. The greatest literature, the greatest songs, the greatest oration: they all have the power to uplift, motivate, heal, encourage, and entertain.

In short, when language is put to constructive use, it communicates everything we value in our lives.

There is a sacredness to language that is eroded when we express ourselves with words meant to take revenge on people, or hurt people, or hate on people.

If we're mindful of what, when, and why we say the things we do, then our words elevate our better angels and become a blessing to whoever is listening.

no. 50

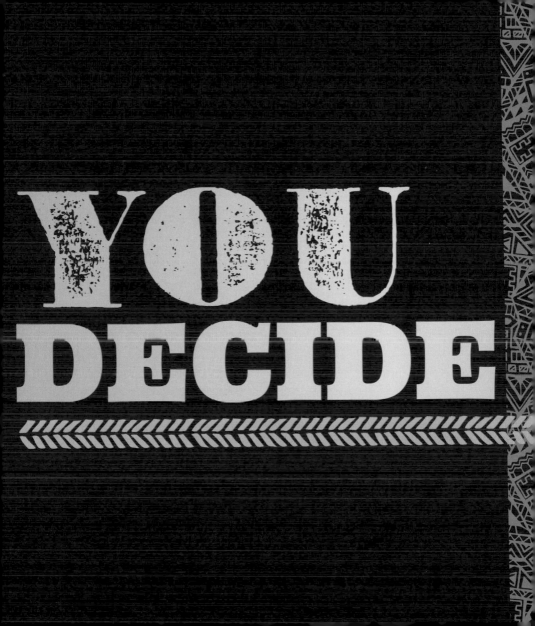

Take a *look*

at any smartphone on the market, and they appear pretty much the same—rectangular, thin, and of a comparable weight.

What makes them truly unique, to each of us, is the software they contain.

We choose between Androids or iPhones, and then we customize them with apps and programs to make each phone unique to us. I'd venture to say that phone companies spend far more time working on what's going to be on the inside of the phone than what's on the outside.

Unfortunately, the same can't be said for most people. Despite the fact that the internal makeup of each individual is by far the most important component of our being. The time you spend figuring out

what kind of person you're going to be is what determines the kind of life you're going to live and the legacy you'll leave behind.

Can you imagine how shallow it would be if, at your funeral, all anyone talked about was how great your abs were, or your lovely hair, or how sleek your car looked, or how avant-garde your apartment was? Yet these are the exact things most of us spend our time working on, worrying about, and wishing for.

I'm not suggesting folks should be unconcerned with how they present themselves to the world, or that they shouldn't be able to enjoy the fruits of their success.

What I am saying is that we are so much more than the sum of our possessions and appearance. I'm saying that we have to be just as concerned about our software as we are about our hardware. Indeed, even more so. Your software is the essence of who you are. It's what makes you distinctive in the world. But only if you understand, accept, and embrace the following:

You control your own destiny.

You're in charge.

You decide.

And yet, none of us has a magic wand. We don't have godlike powers to just magically or mystically transform everything into exactly what we want.

One of my favorite movies is *Bruce Almighty*. It stars Jim Carrey as a guy who complains about God so often that God, played by Morgan Freeman, gives him almighty powers just to teach him how difficult it is to run the world. Carrey's character can do almost anything with his powers—except manipulate the free will we as human beings have to decide and control our own destiny. So for all of his powers, he can't magically convince his ex-girlfriend, played by Jennifer Aniston, to take him back.

She was in control of her own destiny.

She was in charge.

She decided.

At times in your life, it may feel like nothing seems to be going your way. Like the cosmic deck is stacked against you. At some point you're going to find yourself in a particular situation where you have no control over any of the variables.

Not to worry.

The one card that you will still have left to play is the most valuable of all: your ability to become whatever kind of person you want to be.

You control your own destiny.

You're in charge.

You decide.

ACKNOWLEDGMENTS

Thanks to the good people at Hay House for their partnership with SmileyBooks.

Special thanks to Louise Hay and Reid Tracey, and to the team that helped to assemble this beautiful text: Perry Crowe, Christy Salinas, Celeste Phillips, and Karla Baker.

Deep appreciation to Colby Hamilton and Wendy Werris for their research and editorial assistance on this book. And to my executive assistant, Kimberly McFarland, for her vital role as manuscript traffic cop on this project.

And, finally, to all my personal friends (too numerous to list here) who over many months were kind enough to read this manuscript and offer insights that proved invaluable. I am eternally grateful.

ABOUT THE AUTHOR

Tavis Smiley is currently the host of the late-night television talk show *Tavis Smiley* on PBS, as well as *The Tavis Smiley Show* from Public Radio International (PRI). He is also the founder of the nonprofit Tavis Smiley Foundation, which has undertaken a $3-million, four-year campaign called "ENDING POVERTY: America's Silent Spaces" in order to alleviate endemic poverty in America. *TIME* magazine named Smiley to its list of "The World's 100 Most Influential People," and he has been honored with a star on the Hollywood Walk of Fame.

We hope you enjoyed this SmileyBooks publication.
If you'd like to receive additional information, please contact:

SMILEYBOOKS

Distributed by Hay House, Inc.,
P.O. Box 5100
Carlsbad, CA 92018-5100

(760) 431-7695 or (800) 654-5126
(760) 431-6948 (fax) or (800) 650-5115 (fax)
www.hayhouse.com® • www.hayfoundation.org

***

Published and distributed in Australia by: Hay House Australia Pty. Ltd.,
18/36 Ralph St., Alexandria NSW 2015 • Phone: 612-9669-4299
Fax: 612-9669-4144 • www.hayhouse.com.au

Published and distributed in the United Kingdom by: Hay House UK, Ltd.,
Astley House, 33 Notting Hill Gate, London W11 3JQ • Phone: 44-20-3675-2450
Fax: 44-20-3675-2451 • www.hayhouse.co.uk

Published and distributed in the Republic of South Africa by: Hay House SA (Pty), Ltd.,
P.O. Box 990, Witkoppen 2068 • info@hayhouse.co.za • www.hayhouse.co.za

Published in India by: Hay House Publishers India,
Muskaan Complex, Plot No. 3, B-2, Vasant Kunj, New Delhi 110 070
Phone: 91-11-4176-1620 • Fax: 91-11-4176-1630 • www.hayhouse.co.in

Distributed in Canada by: Raincoast Books,
2440 Viking Way, Richmond, B.C. V6V 1N2 • Phone: 1-800-663-5714
Fax: 1-800-565-3770 • www.raincoast.com